W9-AZB-075

COUNTRY
100 OF THE BEST

HL HAL LEONARD PUBLISHING CORPORATION

Home Office: 960 East Mark Street Winona MN 55987

National Sales Office: 8112 West Bluemound Road Milwaukee WI 53213

IT'S NOW OR NEVER

Words and Music by
AARON SCHROEDER and WALLY GOLD

Moderately

Chorus

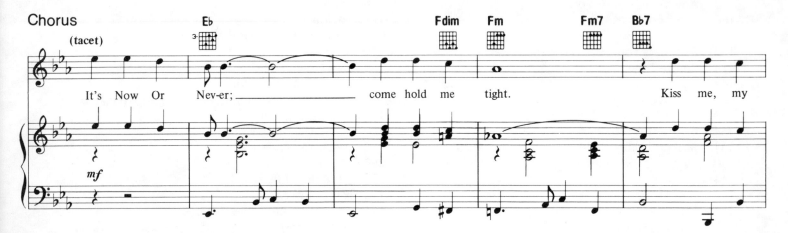

It's Now Or Nev-er; _____ come hold me tight. Kiss me, my

dar-lin'; _____ be mine to-night. _____ To-mor-row

_____ will be too late. _____ It's Now Or Nev-er; _____ my love won't

To Interlude

wait. 1. When I first _____ my love won't wait.
2. Just like a

(opt. octave lower ....)

Fine

Interlude

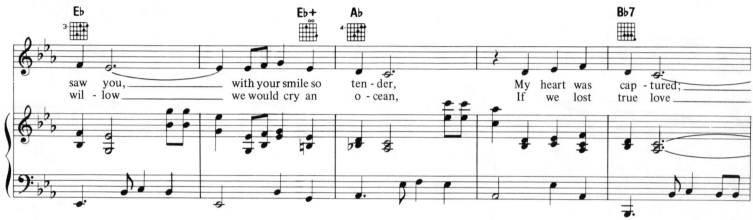

saw you, _____ with your smile so ten-der, My heart was cap-tured;
wil-low _____ we would cry an o-cean, If we lost true love _____

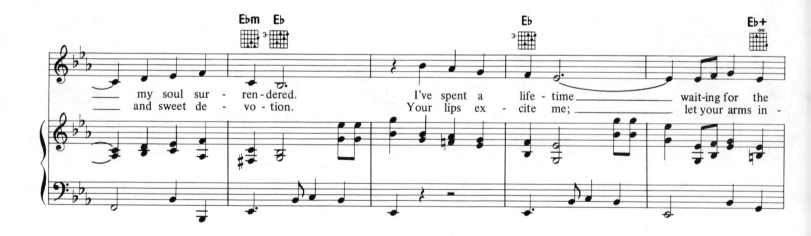

_____ my soul sur-ren-dered. I've spent a life-time _____ wait-ing for the
_____ and sweet de-vo-tion. Your lips ex-cite me; _____ let your arms in-

(Return To Chorus)

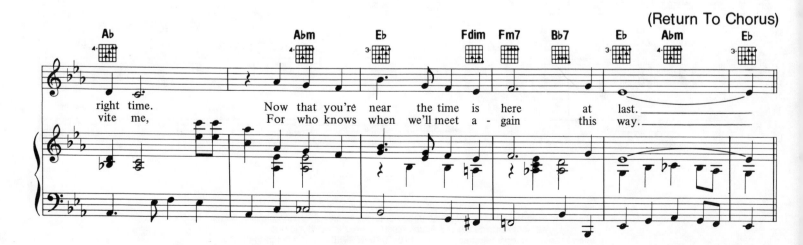

right time. Now that you're near the time is here at last. _____
vite me, For who knows when we'll meet a-gain this way. _____

COLD, COLD HEART

Words and Music by
HANK WILLIAMS

Moderately

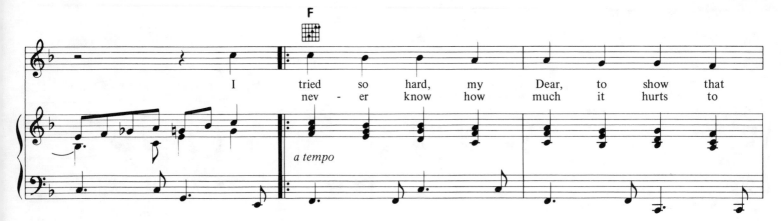

I tried so hard, my Dear, to show that
nev-er know my how much it hurts that

You're my ev-'ry dream
see you sit and cry

Yet you're a-fraid each
You know you need each

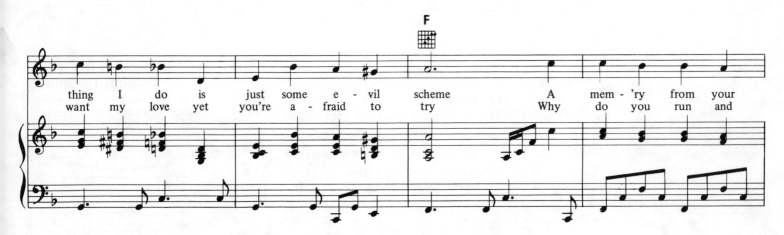

thing I do is just some e-vil scheme   A mem-'ry from your
want my love yet you're a-fraid to try   Why do you run and

lone - some past keeps us so far a - part Why
hide from past life? To try it just ain't smart

can't I free your doubt - ful mind and melt your Cold, Cold
can't I free your doubt - ful mind and melt your Cold, Cold

Heart An - oth - er love be - fore my time made your heart sad and
Heart There was a time when I be - lieved that you be - longed to

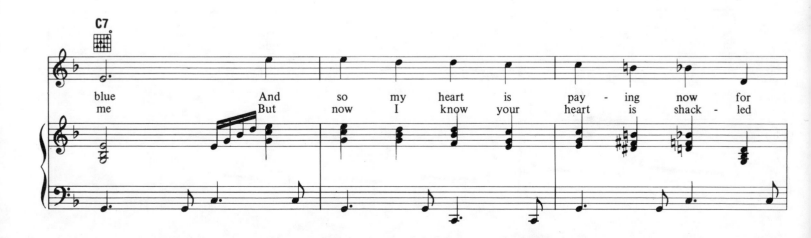

blue And so my heart is pay - ing now for
me But now I know your heart is shack - led

things I did n't do ry
to a mem - o - ry

In an - ger, un - kind
The more I learn to

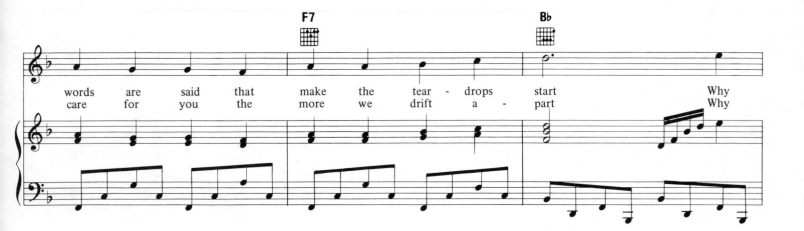

words are said that make the tear - drops start
care for you the more we drift a - part

Why
Why

can't I free your doubt - ful mind and melt your Cold, Cold
can't I free your doubt - ful mind and

Heart.
You'll melt your Cold, Cold Heart.

CAN'T HELP FALLING IN LOVE

Words and Music by
GEORGE WEISS, HUGO PERETTI,
LUIGI CREATORE

Moderately Slow

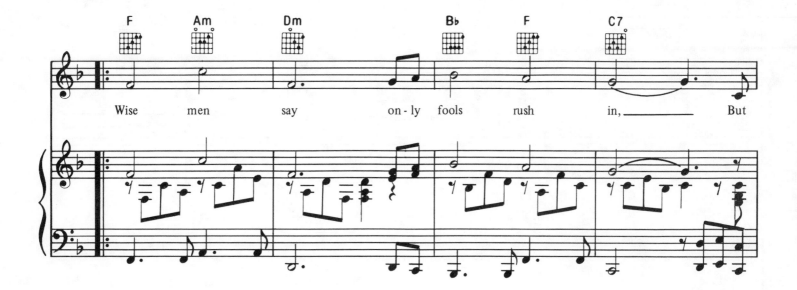

Wise men say on-ly fools rush in, ____ But

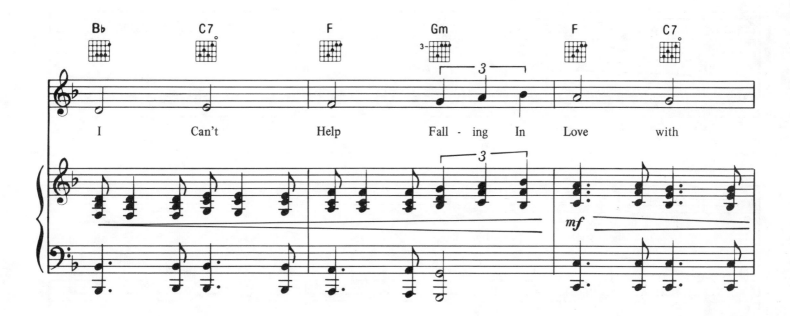

I Can't Help Fall-ing In Love with

8

SOMEBODY'S KNOCKIN'

Words and Music by
ED PENNY and JERRY GILLESPIE

Moderately

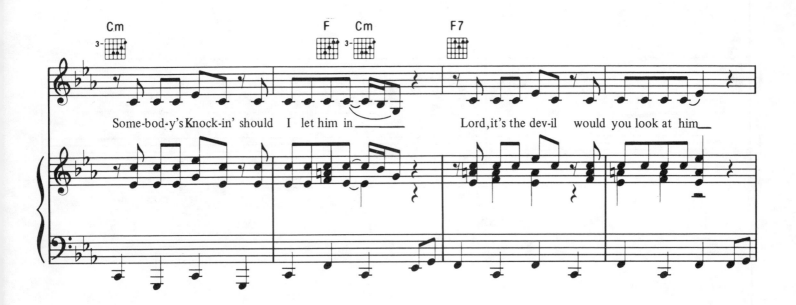

Some-bod-y's Knock-in' should I let him in _____ Lord, it's the dev-il would you look at him __

I've heard a-bout him but I nev-er dreamed __ he'd have blue eyes and blue jeans __

11

ANOTHER SLEEPLESS NIGHT

Words and Music by RORY BOURKE
and CHARLIE BLACK

Lyrics:

The nights have been so lone-ly since you went a-way.

I could not get to sleep try as I may. But now you're back

and you're here to stay.

Still it looks like An-oth-er Sleep-less Night Oh but dar-lin'

15

YOU DON'T KNOW ME

Words and Music by
CINDY WALKER and EDDY ARNOLD

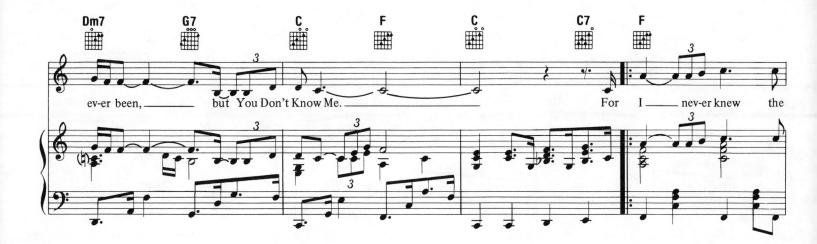

STAND BY ME

Words and Music by
BEN E. KING, JERRY LEIBER
and MIKE STOLLER

Slowly

When the night _____ has come _____ and the land is dark _____ And the moon _____ is the on-ly _____ light we'll see, _____ No, I won't be a-fraid, no _____ I

IT'S HARD TO BE HUMBLE

Words and Music by
MAC DAVIS

Oh Lord It's Hard___ To Be Hum - ble when you're

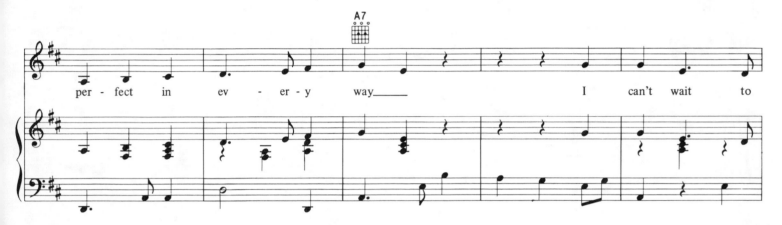

per - fect in ev - er - y way___ I can't wait to

look in___ the mir - ror 'cause I get bet - ter

look - in'___ each_ day___ To___ know me

24

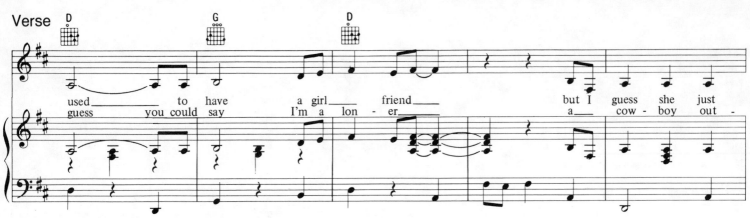

guess they're all_ in awe____ of me
don't e - ven know what that means

Who cares_ I guess

__ it has some-thin'_ to do with the way
I nev - er __ get lone - some ____

that I fill out my
'cause I trea - sure my

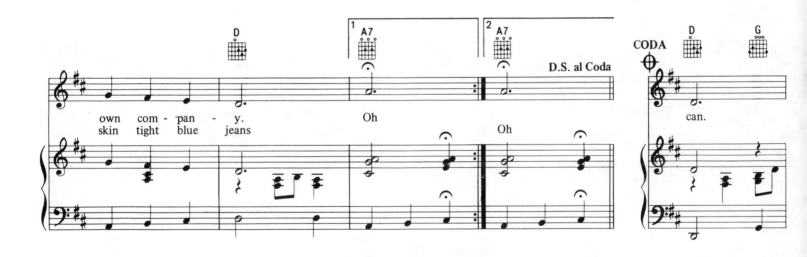

own com - pan - y.
skin tight blue jeans

Oh

D.S. al Coda

Oh

CODA

can.

We're do - in' the best that we can. _____

THROUGH THE YEARS

Words and Music by
STEVE DORFF and MARTY PANZER

Appreciatively

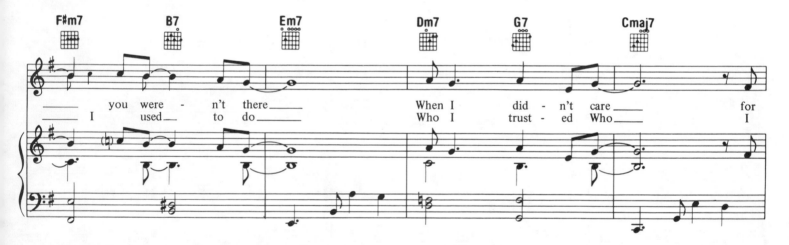

Can't im-a-gine an-y-thing we've missed Can't im-a-gine an-y-thing the
Can't im-a-gine need-ing some-one so But Through The Years it seems to me I

two of us can't do Through The Years You've ne-ver let me
need you more and more Through The Years Through all the good and

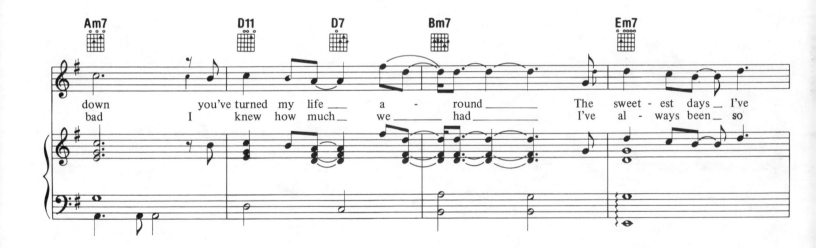

down you've turned my life a-round The sweet-est days I've
bad I knew how much we had I've al-ways been so

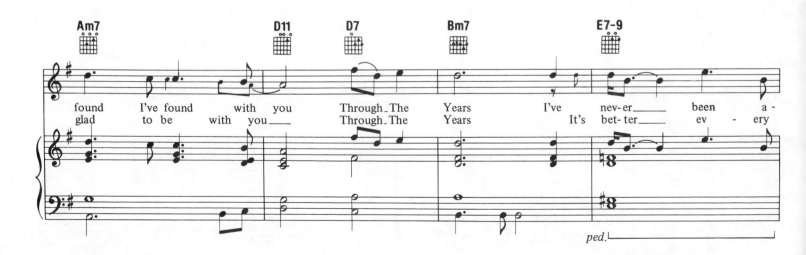

found I've found with you Through The Years I've nev-er been a-
glad to be with you Through The Years It's bet-ter ev-ery

ped.

BY THE TIME I GET TO PHOENIX

Words and Music by
JIM WEBB

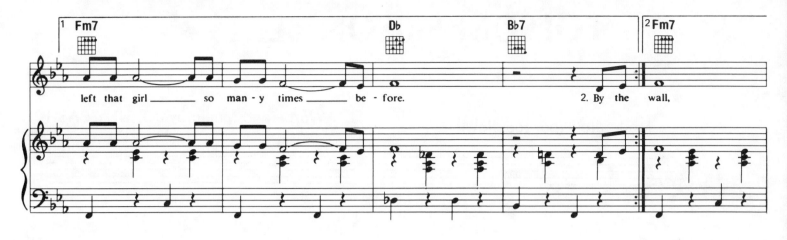

left that girl _____ so man-y times _____ be-fore. 2. By the wall,

that's all. 3. By the

D.S. al Coda

CODA

time and time _____

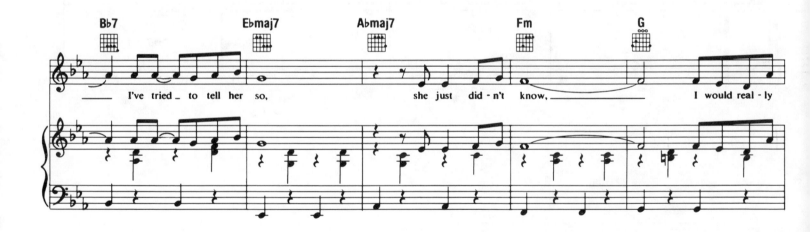

_____ I've tried _ to tell her so, she just did-n't know, _____ I would real-ly

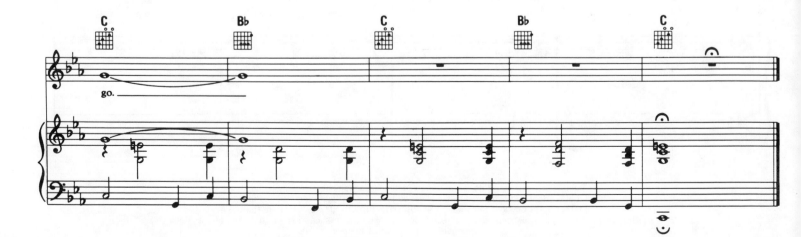

go. _____

FOLSOM PRISON BLUES

Moderately (not too slow)

Words and Music by JOHNNY CASH

hear the train a - com - in'; it's roll - in' 'round the bend, And
I was just a ba - by my ma - ma told me son,_____

I ain't seen the sun - shine since I don't know when. I'm
al - ways be a good boy; don't ev - er play with guns." But I

3. I bet there's rich folks eatin' in a fancy dining car.
They're prob'ly drinkin' coffee and smokin' big cigars,
But I know I had it comin', I know I can't be free,
But those people keep a-movin', and that's what tortures me.

4. Well, if they freed me from this prison, if that railroad train was mine,
I bet I'd move on over a little farther down the line,
Far from Folsom Prison, that's where I want to stay,
And I'd let that lonesome whistle blow my blues away.

YOUR CHEATIN' HEART

By HANK WILLIAMS

Moderately

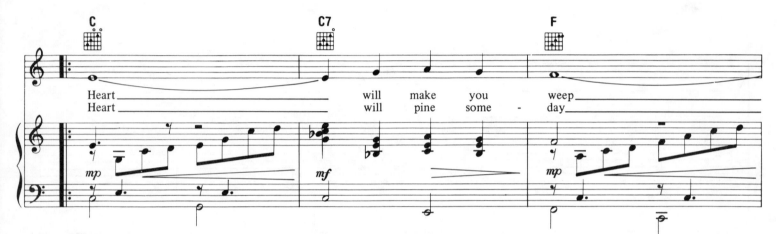

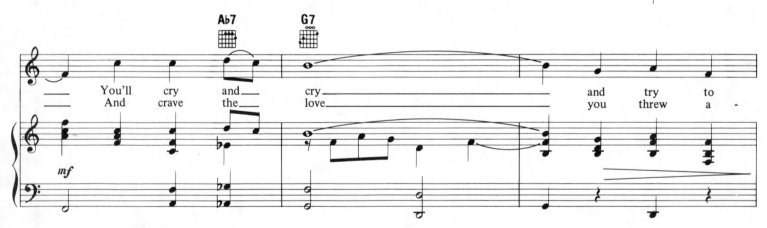

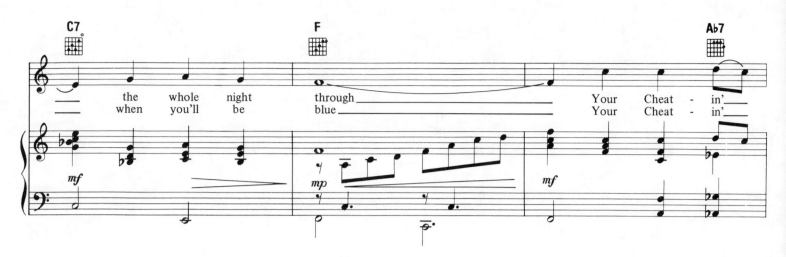

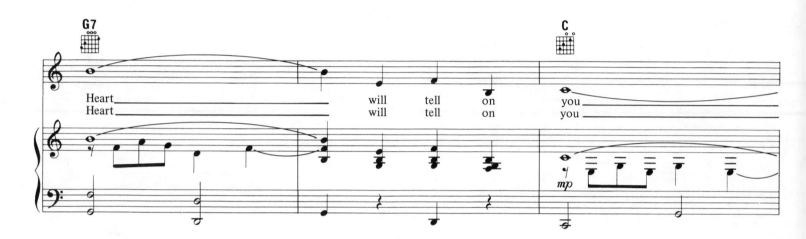

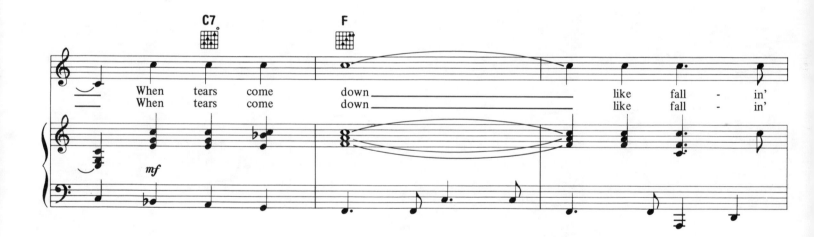

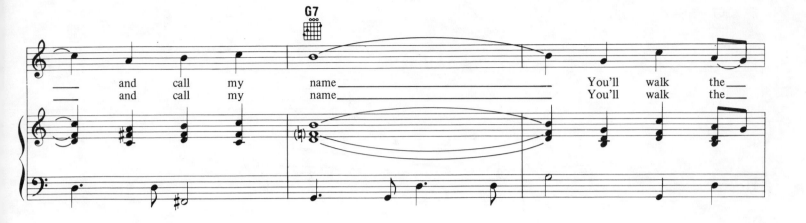

and call my name_____ You'll walk the____
and call my name_____ You'll walk the____

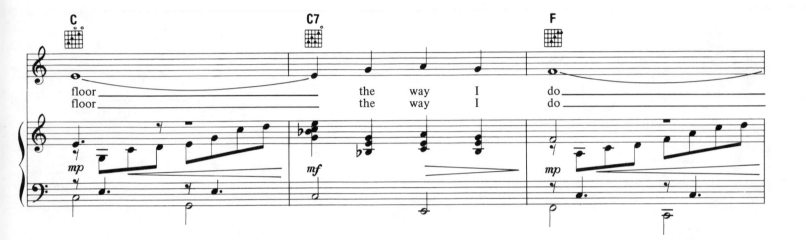

floor_____ the way I do_____
floor_____ the way I do_____

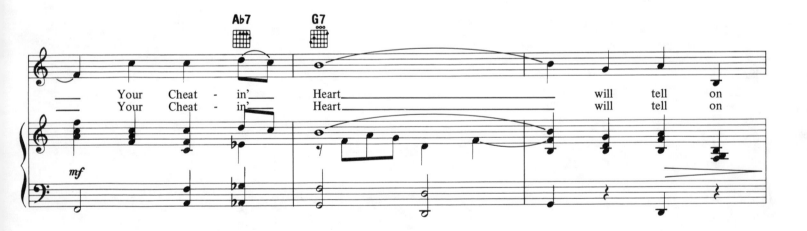

Your Cheat - in'___ Heart_____ will tell on
Your Cheat - in'___ Heart_____ will tell on

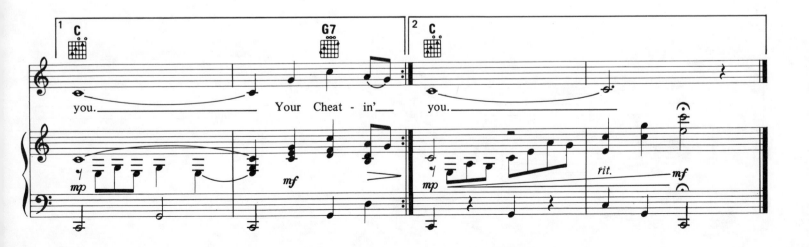

you._____ Your Cheat - in'__ you._____

MOUNTAIN OF LOVE

Moderately Slow

Words and Music by HAROLD DORMAN

Standing on a moun-tain look-ing down on a ci-ty, the way___ I___ feel___ is a
Way___ down be-low ___ there's a half mil-lion peo-ple, some-where there's a church___ with a

dog-gone pi-ty. Tear-drops fal-ling down a moun-tain-side.
big tall stee-ple. In-side the church, there's an al-tar filled with flow-ers.

Man-y times I've been here, Man-y times I've cried.___ We used to be so hap-py,
Wed-ding bells are ring-ing and they should have been ours.___ That's why I'm so lone-ly my

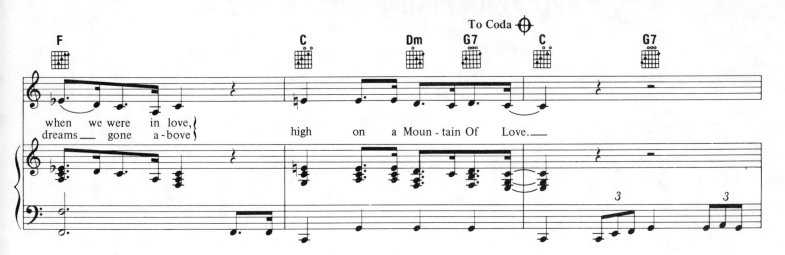

when we were in love,}
dreams __ gone a-bove}
high on a Moun-tain Of Love. __

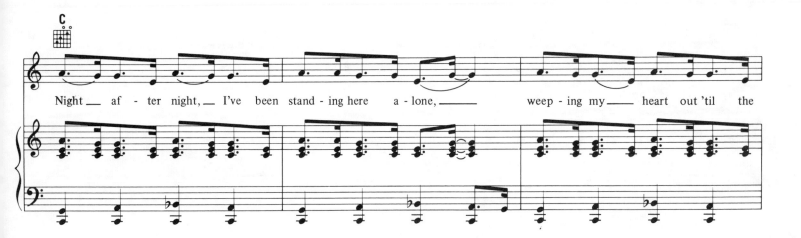

Night __ af-ter night, __ I've been stand-ing here a-lone, _____ weep-ing my __ heart out 'til the

cold gray dawn, _____ pray-ing that you're lone-ly and you'll come here too,

hop-ing just by chance __ that I'll get a glimpse of you. _____ Try-ing hard to find you, __

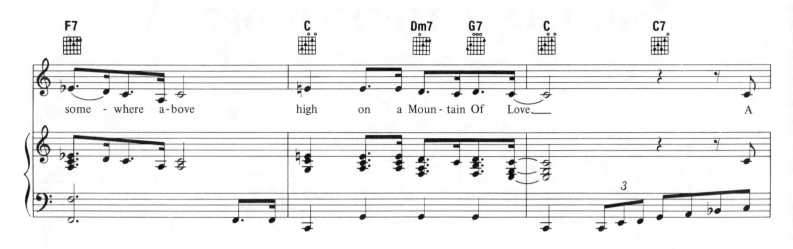

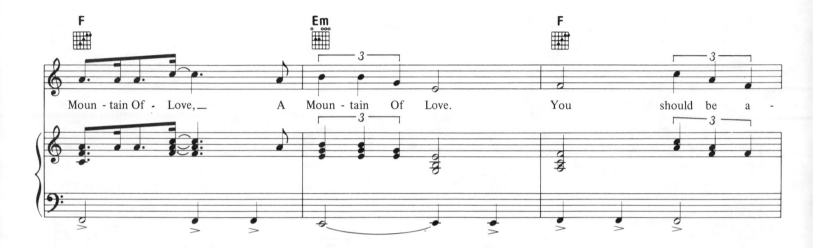

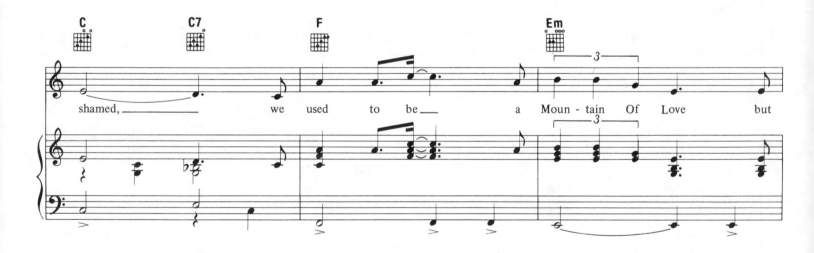

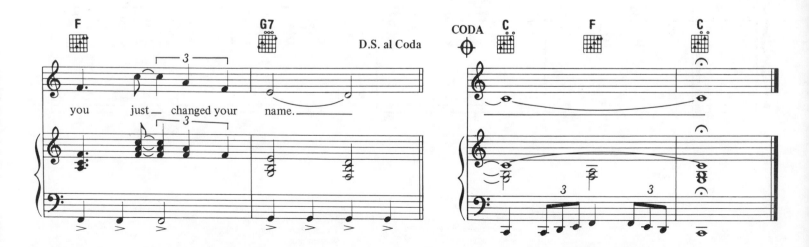

ALL I HAVE TO DO IS DREAM

By BOUDLEAUX BRYANT

Moderately

Dream, _____ dream, dream, dream, _____ Dream, _____ dream, dream, dream.__ When

I want you _____ in my arms, When I want you _____ and all your charms When
I feel blue _____ in the night, And I need you _____ to hold me tight When

WALKING THE FLOOR OVER YOU

Words and Music by
ERNEST TUBB

1. You left me and you____ went a way____
2. (Now,) Dar - ling, you know I love you well____
3. (Now,) some - day you may be lone - some too____

You said that you'd be back in just a day____
Love you more than I can ev - er tell____
Walk - ing the floor is good for you____

HEY, GOOD LOOKIN'

Words and Music by
HANK WILLIAMS

Moderately

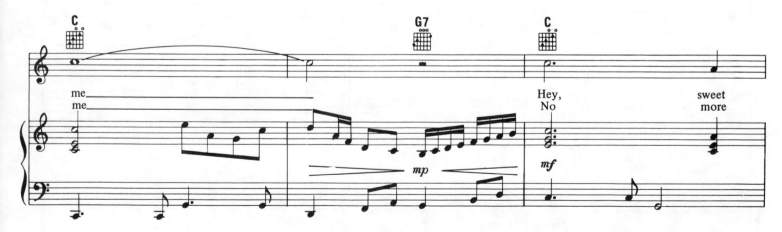

ba - by, I

look - in',

Don't _____ you think may - be

know _____ I've been took - en

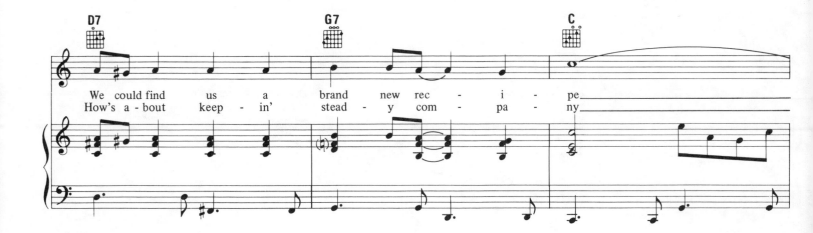

D7

G7

C

We could find us a brand new rec - i - pe _____

How's a - bout keep - in' stead - y com - pa - ny _____

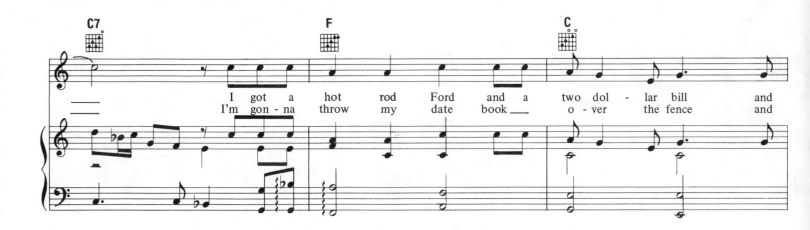

C7

F

C

I got a hot rod Ford and a two dol - lar bill and

I'm gon - na throw my date book _____ o - ver the fence and

F

C

F

I know a spot right o - ver the hill _____ There's so - da pop and the

find me _____ one right for five or ten cents _____ I'll keep it 'til it's _____

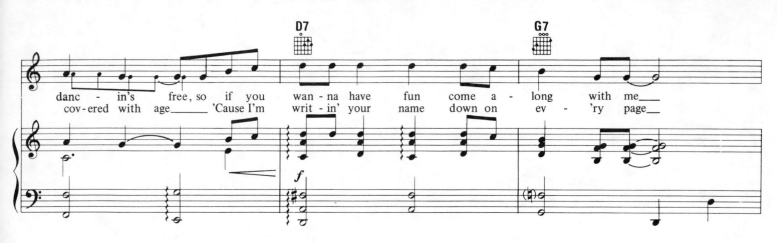

danc - in's free, so if you wan - na have fun come a - long with me___
cov - ered with age___ 'Cause I'm writ - in' your name down on ev - 'ry page___

Hey, Good Look-in' What - cha got cook-in'
Hey, Good Look-in' What - cha got cook-in'

How's a - bout cook - in' some - thin' up with me.___
How's a - bout cook - in' some - thin' up with

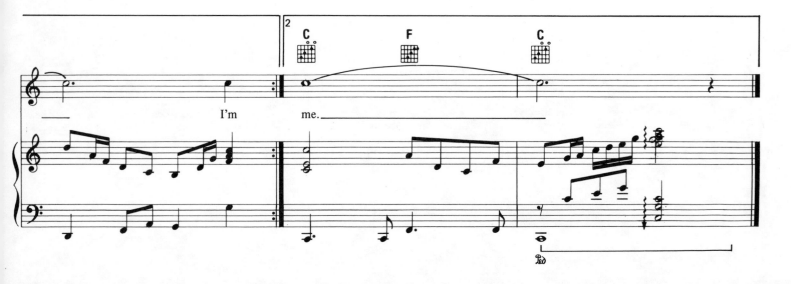

I'm me.___

KISS AN ANGEL GOOD MORNIN'

Moderately

By BEN PETERS

1. When
2. (Well)

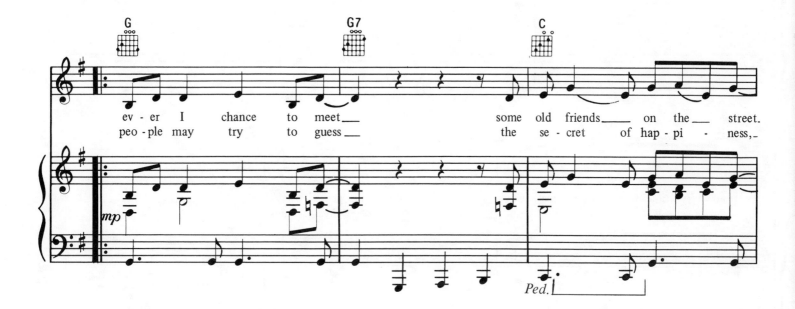

ev - er I chance to meet___ some old friends___ on the___ street.
peo - ple may try to guess___ the se - cret of hap - pi - ness,___

___ They won - der how does a man___ get to be this way..
___ But some of them nev - er learn,___ it's a sim - ple thing..

FADED LOVE

Words and Music by
JOHN WILLS and BOB WILLS

Moderato

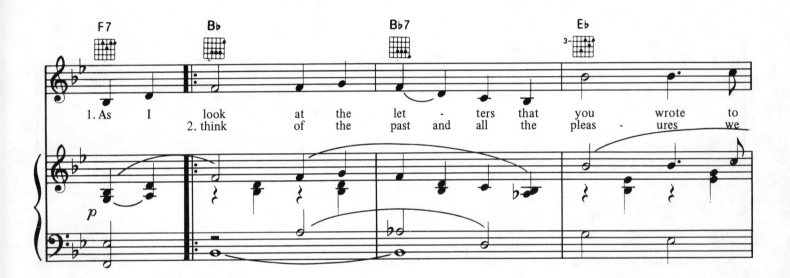

1. As I look at the let - ters that you wrote to
2. think of the past and all the pleas - ures we

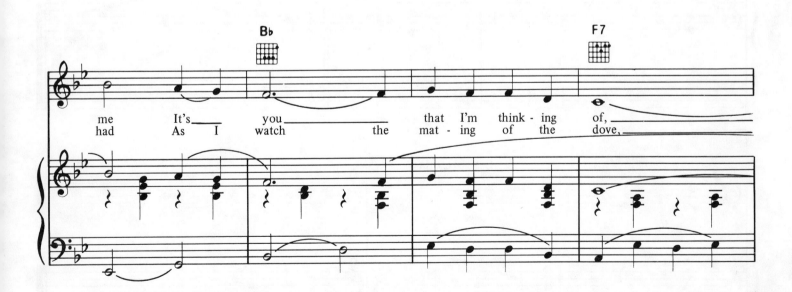

me It's____ you_____ that I'm think - ing of,____
had As I watch the mat - ing of the dove,____

53

BAR ROOM BUDDIES

Words and Music by MILTON L. BROWN,
STEPHEN H. DORFF, CLIFF CROFFORD
and SNUFF GARRETT

MIDNIGHT RODEO

Words and Music by DEWAYNE ORENDER
and RODGER WARE

Lively Country feel

Put on__ your new blue jeans__ and we'll dance to - night__
No saw dust on the floor,__ no juke box a round,__

to the songs that we love so.
just my old clock ra - di - o.

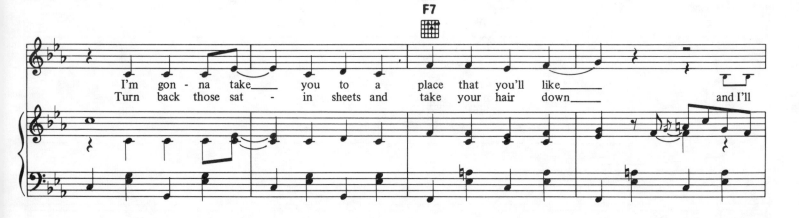

I'm gon - na take__ you to a place that you'll like__ and I'll
Turn back those sat - in sheets and take your hair down__ and I'll

CRYING MY HEART OUT OVER YOU

Words and Music by CARL BUTLER
MARIJOHN WILKIN, LOUISE CERTAIN and GLADYS STACEY

Moderately

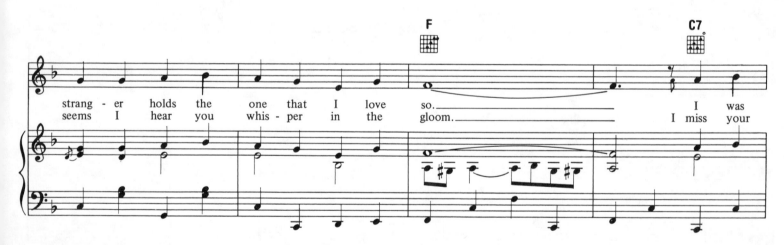

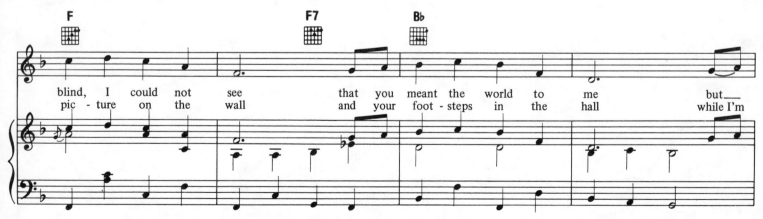

RUBY, DON'T TAKE YOUR LOVE TO TOWN

Words and Music
By MEL TILLIS

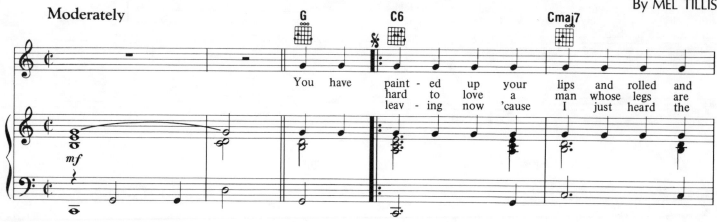

You have paint-ed up your lips and rolled and
hard to love a man whose legs are
leav-ing now 'cause I just heard the

curled your tint-ed hair.
bent and par-a-lized,
slam-ming of a door

And the Ru-by are you con-tem-plat-ing
wants and needs of a wo-man your age.
The way I know I've heard it slam one

go-ing out some-where?
Ru-by I re-a-lize,
hun-dred times be-fore,

The sha-dows on the wall tell me the
But it won't be long I've heard them say un-
And if I could move I'd get my gun and

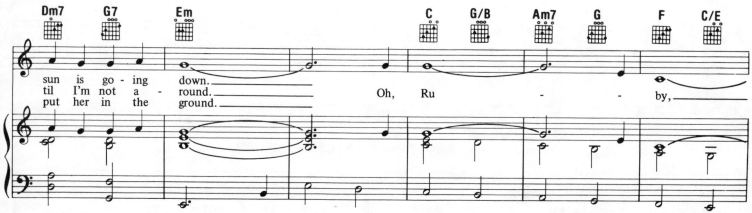

sun is go-ing down.
til I'm not a-round.
put her in the ground.

Oh, Ru -   - by,

I LOVE

By TOM T. HALL

Moderately slow

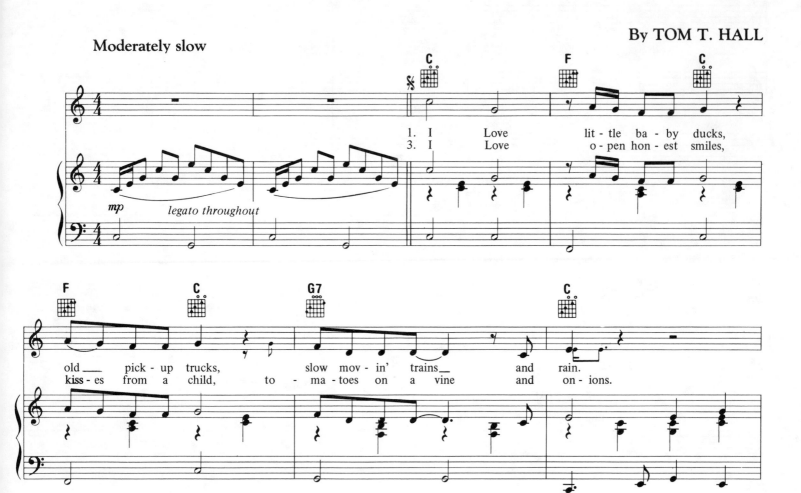

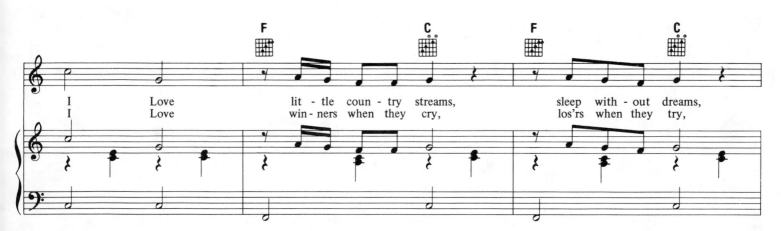

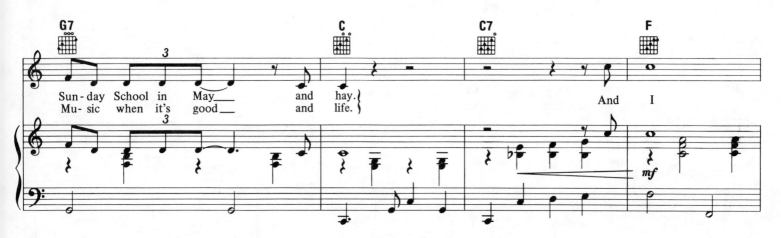

JAMBALAYA
(On The Bayou)

Words and Music by
HANK WILLIAMS

Moderately

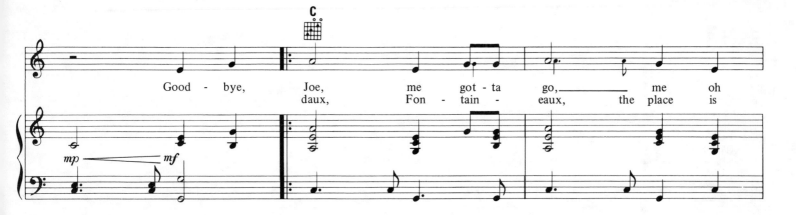

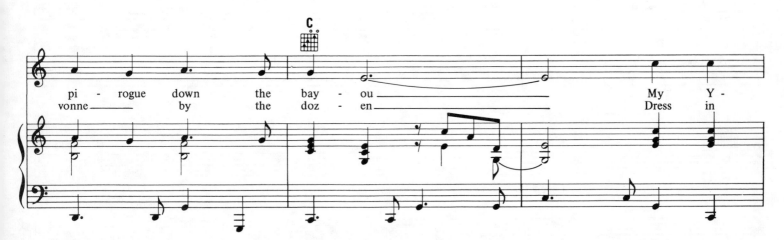

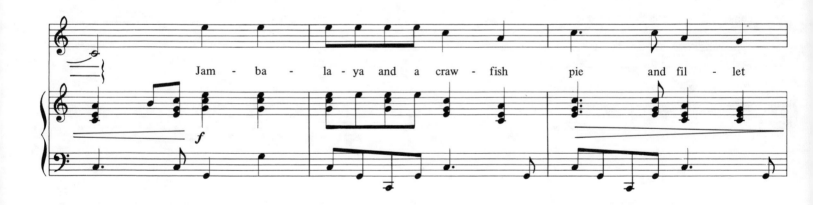

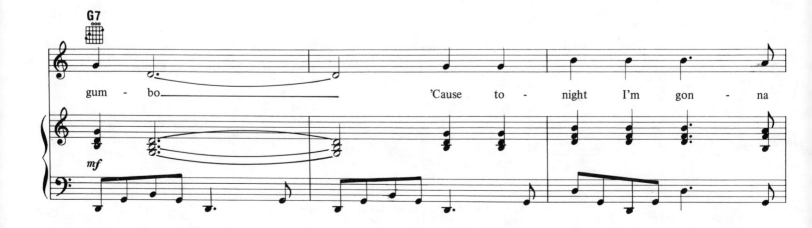

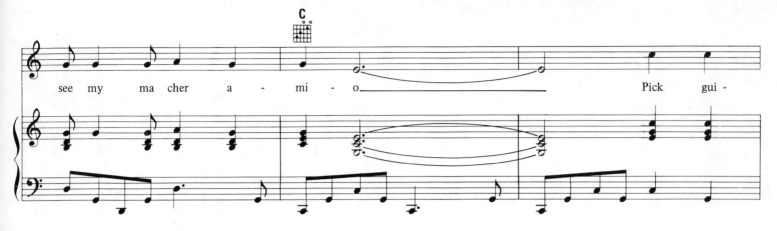

see my ma cher a - mi - o _____ Pick gui-

tar, fill fruit jar and be gay - o _____ Son of a

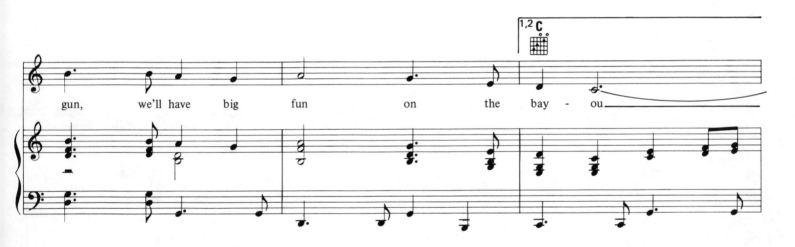

gun, we'll have big fun on the bay - ou _____

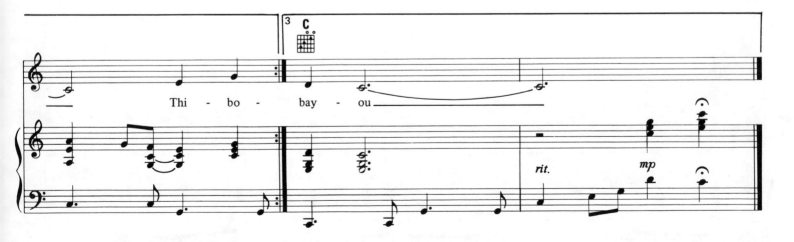

Thi - bo - bay - ou _____

3. Settle down far from town, get me a pirogue
And I'll catch all the fish in the bayou
Swap my mon to buy Yvonne what whe need-o
Son of a gun, we'll have big fun on the bayou

BLESSED ARE THE BELIEVERS

Words and Music by
RORY BOURKE, CHARLIE BLACK
and SANDY PINKARD

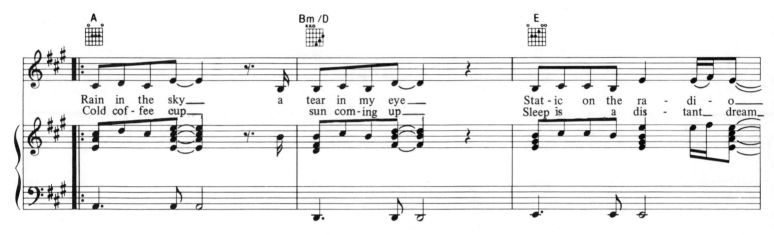

Rain in the sky___ a tear in my eye___ Stat-ic on the ra-di-o___
Cold cof-fee cup___ sun com-ing up___ Sleep is a dis-tant dream___

The long night's be-gun with din-ner for one
Some-thing you said rolls 'round in my head

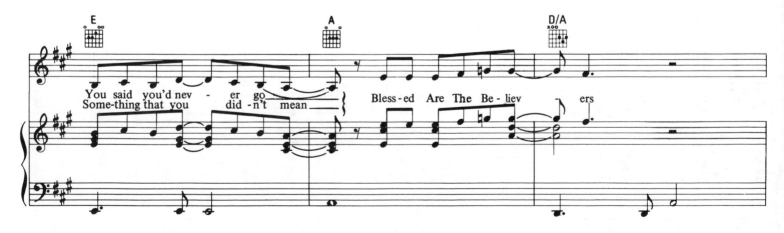

You said you'd nev-er go___ Bless-ed Are The Be-liev-ers
Some-thing that you did-n't mean___

They shall in-her-it a heart___ -ache___ Be-liev-ing in you___

___ babe___ That was my great-est heart -break___

Bless-ed are all the left___ be -hind___ For their hearts___ shall one___

___ day mend___ When love and those same___ sweet lies___

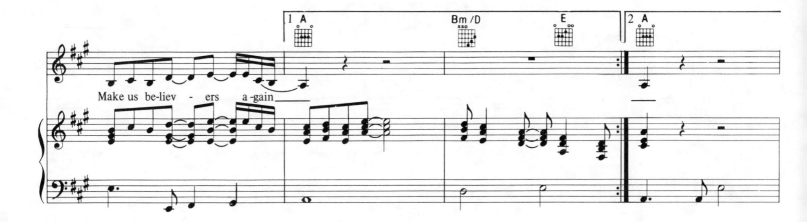

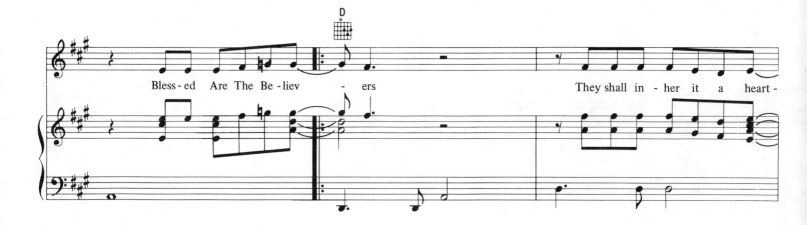

Make us be-liev - ers a-gain___

Bless - ed Are The Be -liev - ers___ They shall in - her it a heart-

ache___ Be - liev -ing in you _____ Babe ___

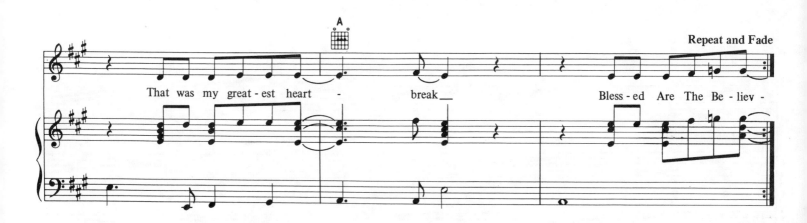

Repeat and Fade

That was my great-est heart - break___ Bless - ed Are The Be -liev -

PLAY SOMETHING WE COULD LOVE TO

Medium Country

Words and Music by DIANE PFEIFER

Hel - lo_____ do you take re - quests?_ There's some - thing that I'd like._ What you've
it's a lot to ask,____ from some - one you don't know.. But I

played so far,_ on the ra - di - os fine,_ but I don't feel like dan - cin' to - night. And he's get - tin' rea - dy to go,_ but
had to turn_ some - where for help_ 'cause I just____ don't want him to go. So please, can I count on you_ to

you could_ change his mind._ Please, won't you help me out this time?}
play me_ some - thing nice. Please, help me make him stay to - night.}

Play Some-thing We Could

Love_ To. One that just goes on_____ and on.. Some-thing slow_ and sim - ple____ and I can keep him

close so long.___ And when the song is o - ver, _____ there's one more thing ___ you could do. Would you

play it a-gain, _____ the whole night through._   I know_

through_   Well thanks   now I got-ta get back_ be - fore he knows I phoned_   now it's

up to you _ to keep me from be-ing a - lone.   Play Some-thing We Could

through._

BEFORE I MET YOU

Words and Music by CHARLES L. SEITZ,
JOE "CANNONBALL" LEWIS and BILL DENNY

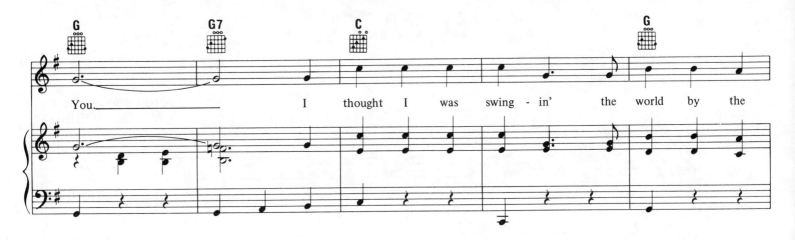

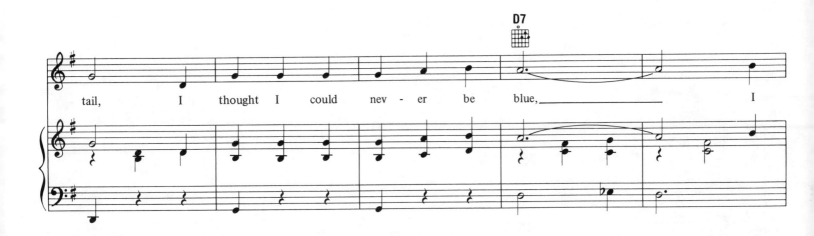

EL PASO

Words and Music by
MARTY ROBBINS

Moderato

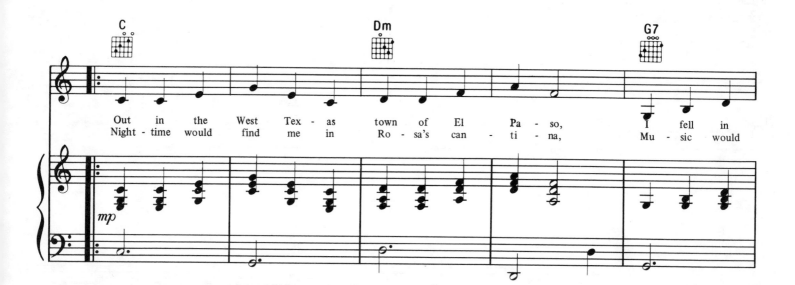

Out in the West Tex - as town of El Pa - so, I fell in
Night - time would find me in Ro - sa's can - ti - na, Mu - sic would

love with a Mex - i - can girl.
play and Fe - li - na would

whirl.

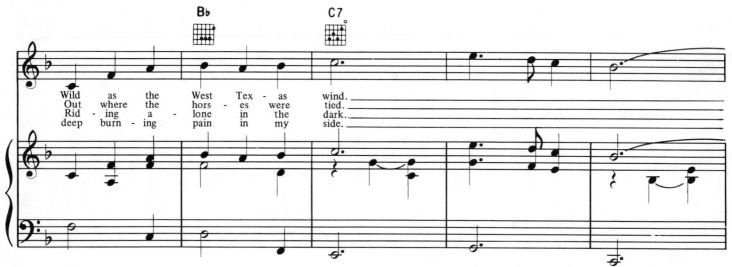

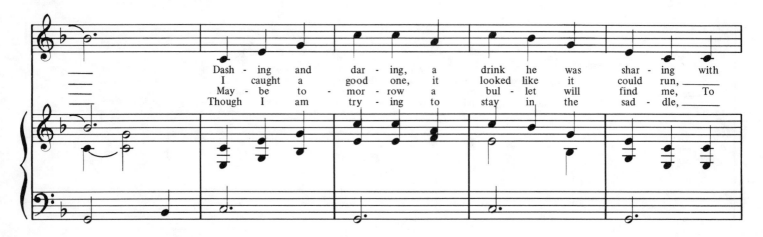

STILL DOIN' TIME

Words and Music by MICHAEL P. HEENEY
and JOHN E. MOFFAT

Country Waltz style

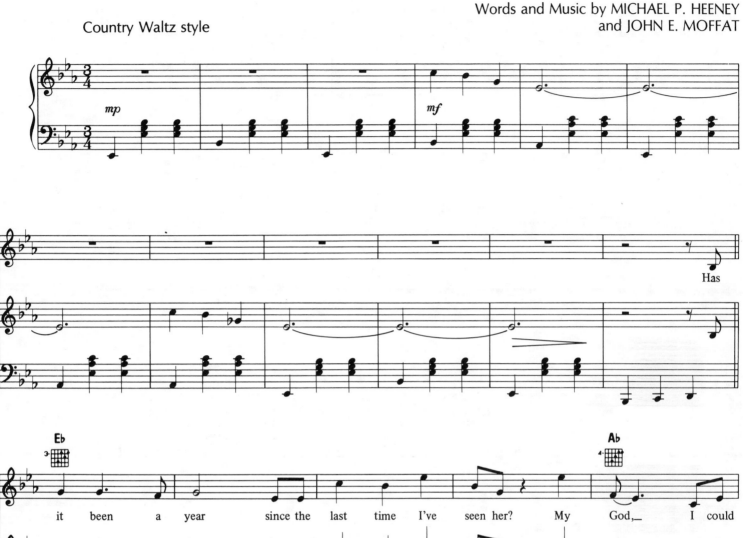

Has it been a year since the last time I've seen her? My God,__ I could

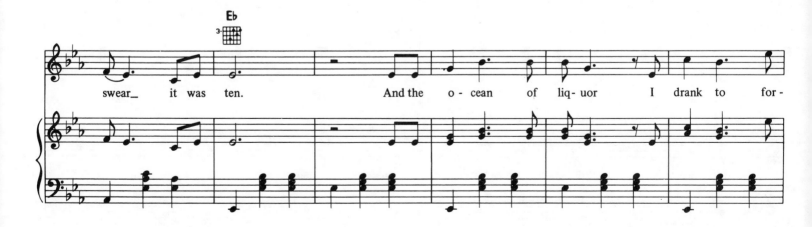

swear__ it was ten. And the o- cean of liq- uor I drank to for-

My poor heart is break-ing, but there's no es - cap-ing; each

morn-ing___ I wake up and I find.___ Still Do - in' Time.___

Oh, when you're

Still Do - in' Time.___

LET'S DO SOMETHING CHEAP AND SUPERFICIAL

Words and Music by RICHARD E. LEVINSON

Medium Country Shuffle

1. Though your

hair is all___ in tang - les and your make-up is a mess,___ though most of what you're drink-ing___ is

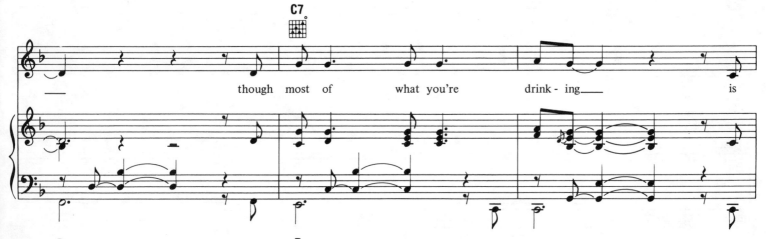

spill-ing down___ your dress.___ And to keep from fall-ing off___

Chorus

2. You've got lipstick showing on your teeth and a run down your hose,
   and where you got that cheap perfume, well God only knows.
   Now I'll be glad to have you home long before daylight,
   the sun is your worst enemy, thank God it's dark tonight.

(CHORUS)

HEARTBREAKER

Words and Music by
CAROLE BAYER SAGER
& DAVID WOLFERT

Moderately

Here I sit all a - lone think - in' 'bout what I

should have known. You made me think that I could need _____ you

ANY WHICH WAY YOU CAN

Words and Music by MILTON L. BROWN,
STEPHEN H. DORFF
and SNUFF GARRETT

Moderately Slow

1. It's hard for a back street af-fair to be eas-y, for each hour of hap-pi-ness there's two hours of pain. But we meet in the shad-ows be-cause all that mat-ters is spend-ing the night with each oth-er a-gain. You'll

and I've got__ mine. I know you can nev- er be free, And

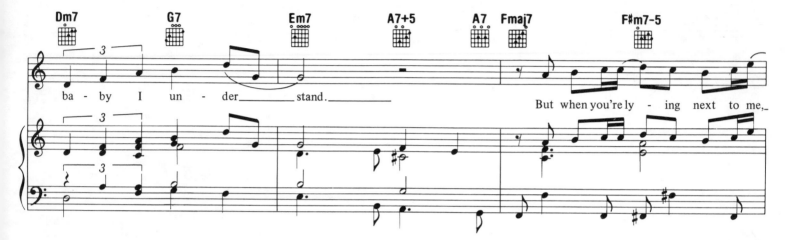

ba - by I un - der_____ stand._____ But when you're ly - ing next to me,__

_____ just love me An - y Which Way You__ Can.

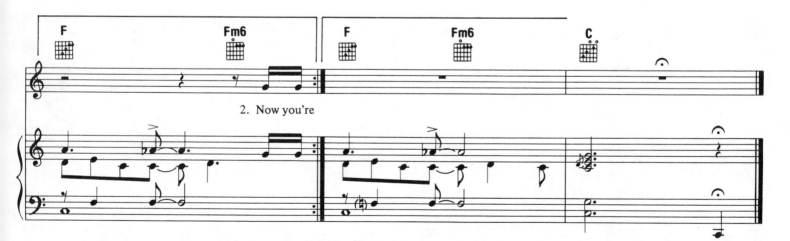

2. Now you're

2. Now you're on your way home leavin' me all alone,
feeling almost as empty as this big double bed.
And it's hard to be strong when I know I belong
in your arms, but I'm lying here lonely instead.

SHADOWS IN THE MOONLIGHT

Words and Music by
CHARLIE BLACK and RORY BOURKE

We'll be Shad - ows In The Moon - light,
a lit - tle hide - a - way
dar - ling, I'll meet
where we can love

you at mid - night,
the whole night a - way
we'll be Shad - ows In The Moon - light

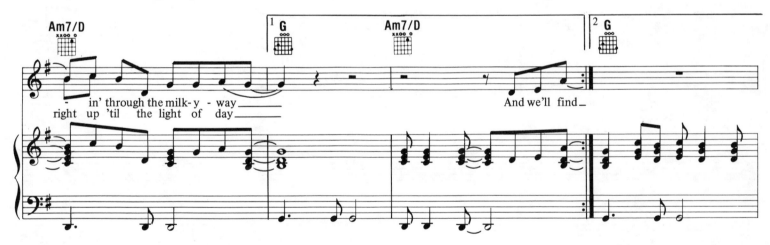

- in' through the milk - y - way
right up 'til the light of day
And we'll find

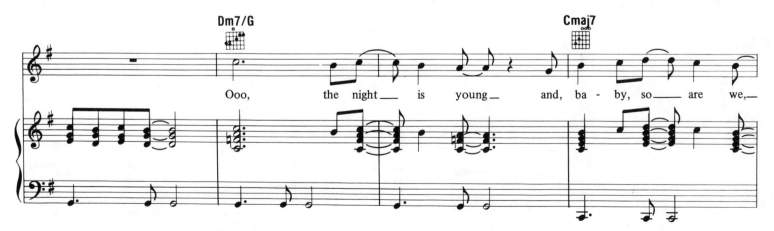

Ooo, the night is young and, ba - by, so are we,

COWBOYS AND CLOWNS

Words and Music by STEPHEN H. DORFF,
SNUFF GARRETT, LARRY HERBSTRITT
and GARY HARJU

Moderately slow, with expression

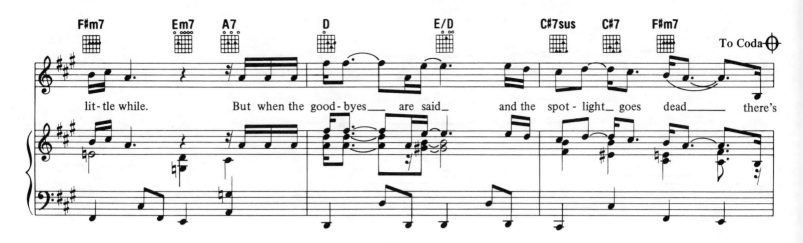

lit-tle while. But when the good-byes___ are said___ and the spot-light___ goes dead_____ there's

no-one left__ who cares__ to hang a- round___ to love the Cow-boys And Clowns.

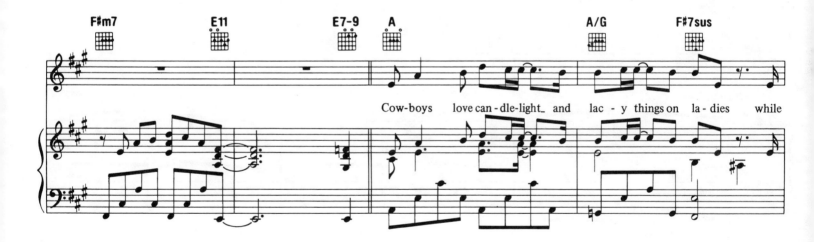

Cow-boys love can-dle-light___ and lac - y things on la - dies while

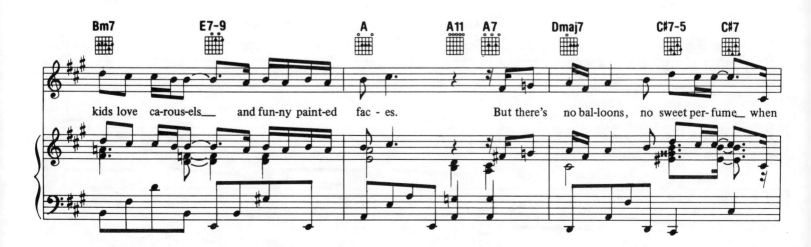

kids love ca-rous-els___ and fun-ny paint-ed fac - es. But there's no bal-loons, no sweet per-fume__ when

mid-night brings you down,_ no-one to hold you close_when the morn-in' comes_ a - round. Ev-'ry- bod - y

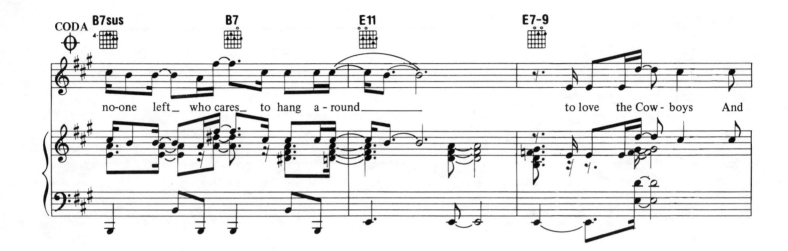

no-one left_ who cares_ to hang a - round_____ to love the Cow - boys And

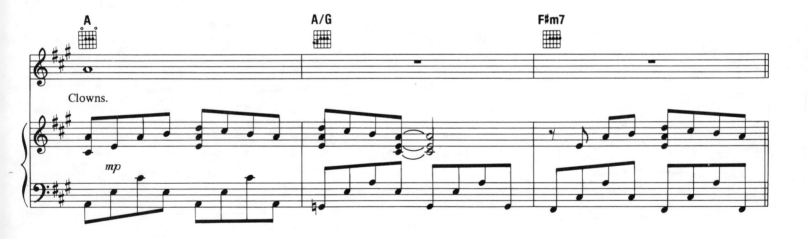

Clowns.

Cow-boys And Clowns._

WHAT ARE WE DOIN' IN LOVE

Words and Music by
RANDY GOODRUM

THE END OF THE WORLD

Words by SYLVIA DEE
Music by ARTHUR KENT

Slowly

Why does the sun go on shin - ing? Why does the sea rush to shore? Don't they know it's The

End Of The World, 'Cause you don't love me an - y more? Why do the birds go on

sing - ing? Why do the stars glow a - bove? Don't they know it's The

(I'm Gonna)
PUT YOU BACK ON THE RACK

Vigorous Country Rock

Words and Music by RANDY GOODRUM
and BRENT MAHER

Well it don't take much_ to change your mind_ Just a lit-tle skim-py skirt and a lit-tle bit of wine I'm

tired of stay-ing up a los-ing sleep So I've got some-thing to tell_ you that just won't keep I'm Gon-na

Put You Back On The Rack_ Trade you in_ and get my mon-ey back_

Cause I've got a life-time guar-en-tee_ Says you be-long to_ me I'm gon-na

D.S. al Coda

lit -tle bit of lov - in' that ain't ask-ing too much Cause if you don't I'm gon-na pack you up I'm gon -na

CODA F

I guess you're just too blind to — see — You ain't fool-in'

me —

(Spoken) Well it won't take much to change your style Just

stay at home just every once in a - while A little bit of lovin' Now is that asking too much Cause if you don't

107

GONE

Words and Music by
SMOKEY ROGERS

Slowly

Chorus

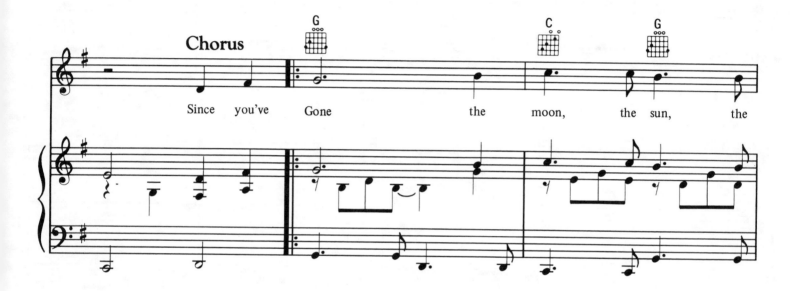

Since you've Gone the moon, the sun, the

stars in the sky know the rea-son why__ I cry.

WOODEN HEART

Words and Music by
FRED WISE, BEN WEISMAN,
KAY TWOMEY and BERTHOLD KAEMPFERT

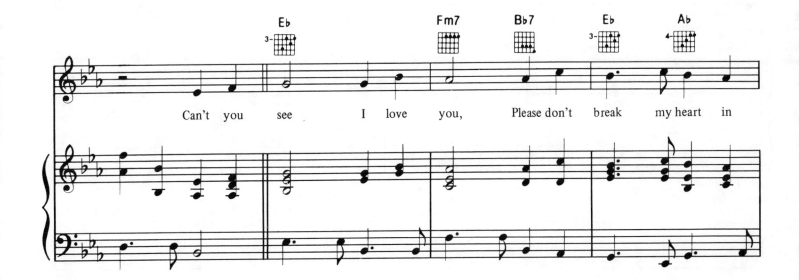

Can't you see I love you, Please don't break my heart in

two, That's not hard to do, 'Cause I don't have a

BYE BYE, LOVE

Words and Music by FELICE BRYANT
and BOUDLEAUX BRYANT

Moderately fast

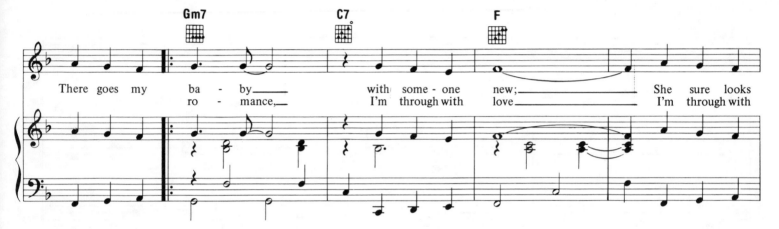

There goes my ba—by____ with some-one new;____ She sure looks
ro—mance,____ I'm through with love____ I'm through with

hap-py;____ I sure am blue;____ She was my ba—by____
count-ing____ the stars a-bove;____ And here's the rea-son

____ till he stepped in;____ Good-bye to ro—mance____
that I'm so free;____ My lo-vin' ba—by____

(Let's Get)
DIXIEFRIED

Words and Music by CARL PERKINS

Rock-A-Billy style

(2nd time)

Well, on the

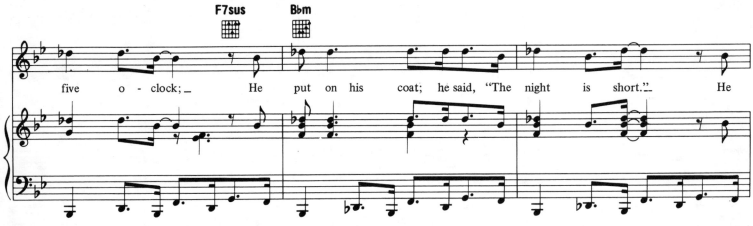

out - skirts of town there's a lit - tle night spot;_ the Dan dropped_ in a - bout

five o - clock;_ He put on his coat; he said, "The night is short." He

reached in his pock - et and he flashed a quart.__ He hol - lered, "Rave_____ on,

chil - dren I'm with you!" "Rave ___ on, cats!" He cried, ___ "It's

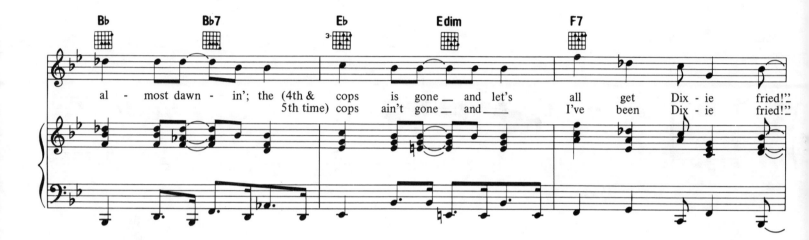

al - most dawn - in'; the (4th & cops is gone ___ and let's all get Dix - ie fried!"
5th time) cops ain't gone ___ and ___ I've been Dix - ie fried!"

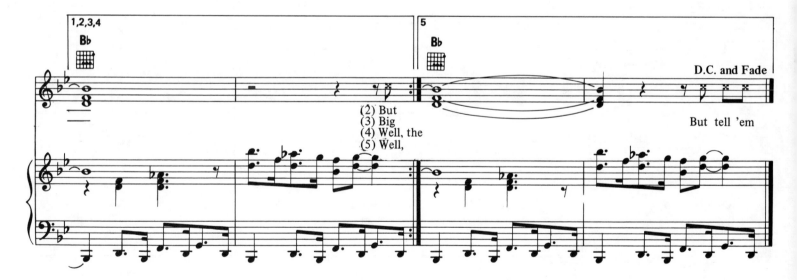

(2) But
(3) Big
(4) Well, the
(5) Well,

D.C. and Fade

But tell 'em

2. But Dan got happy and he started ravin'
   He checked out a razor but he wasn't shavin'
   And all the cats knew the job'd been hot
   He was borned and raised in a butcher shop! (Chorus)

3. Big LeRoy Brown was a-sittin' on a stool
   He made a bad, bad error when he called Dan a fool
   The junk yard dog was layin' flat on the ground
   Dan was a-smilin' and out jumpin' around. (Chorus)

ANY TIME

Words and Music by
HERBERT HAPPY LAWSON

Moderately

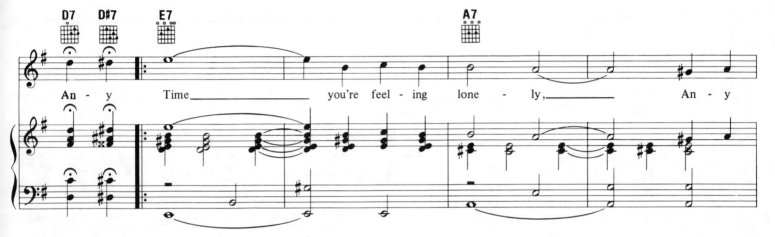

Any Time you're feel-ing lone-ly, Any

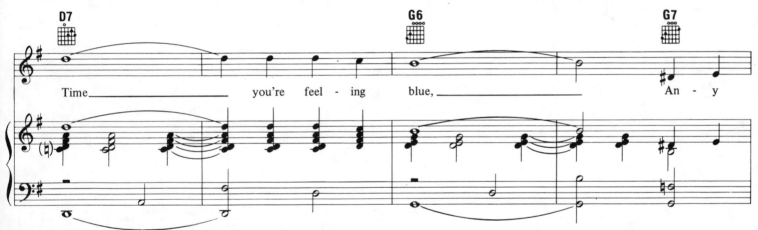

Time you're feel-ing blue, Any

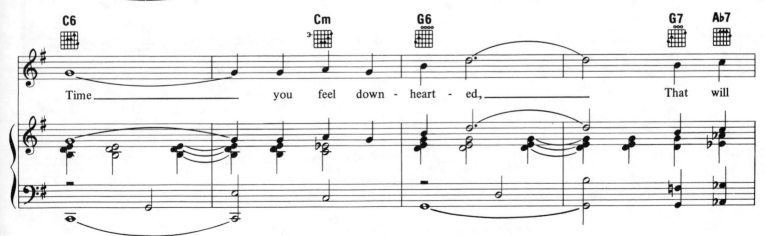

Time you feel down-heart-ed, That will

WATERLOO

Words and Music by JOHN LOUDERMILK
and MARIJOHN WILKIN

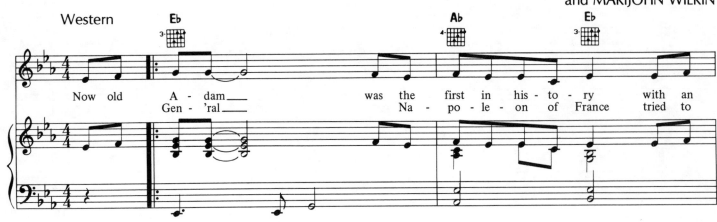

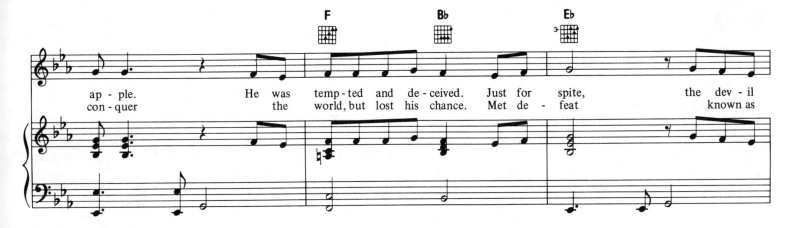

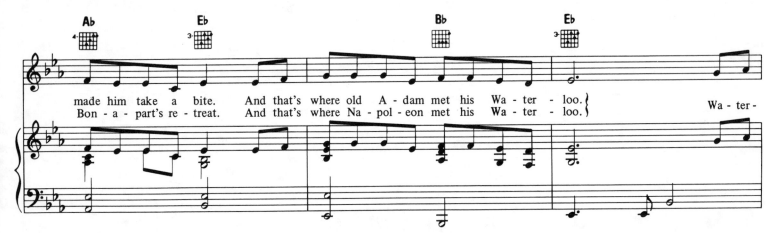

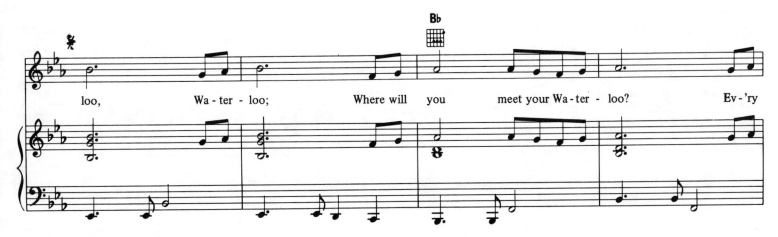

pup-py has it's day ev-'ry bo-dy has to pay. Ev-'ry bo-dy has to meet his Wa-ter - loo. Lit-tle

loo. Now a fel-lah who's dar-lin' proved un-true. Took her life but

he lost his too. Now he swings where the lit-tle bird-ies sing, and that's

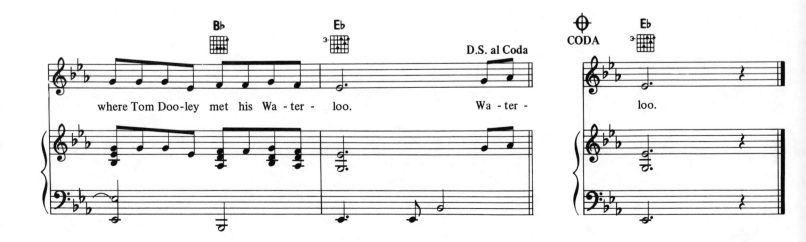

where Tom Doo-ley met his Wa-ter - loo. Wa-ter - loo.

FREE TO BE LONELY AGAIN

Words and Music by DIANE PFEIFER

Easy Country two-beat

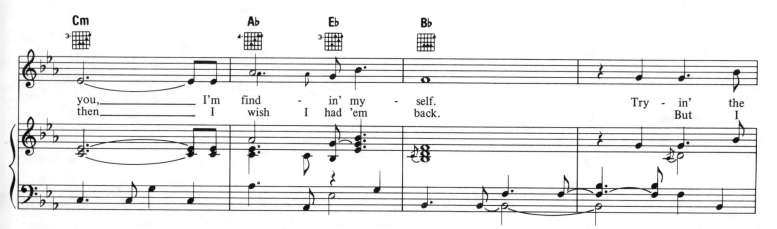

ROCKY TOP

Words and Music by
BOUDLEAUX BRYANT and
FELICE BRYANT

Wish that I was on ol' Rock-y Top,
Once two stran - gers climbed ol' Rock-y Top,

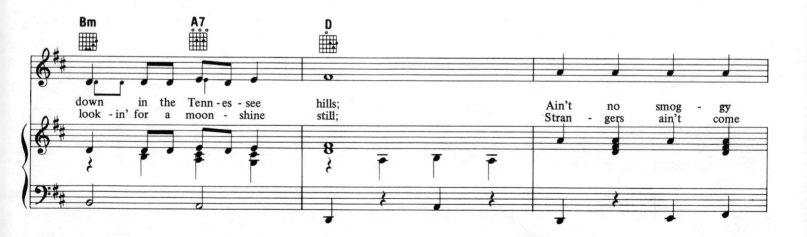

down in the Tenn-es-see hills; Ain't no smog-gy
look-in' for a moon-shine still; Stran - gers ain't come

G D Bm A7
smoke on Rock - y Top; Ain't no tel - e - phone
down from Rock - y Top; Reck - on they nev - er
D G D
bills; Once I had a girl on Rock - y Top;
will; Corn won't grow at all on Rock - y Top;
Bm A7 D
Half bear, oth - er half cat; Wild as a mink, but
Dirt's too rock - y by far; That's why all the
G D Bm A7 D
sweet as sod - a pop, I still dream a - bout that;
folks on Rock - y Top get their corn from a - jar;

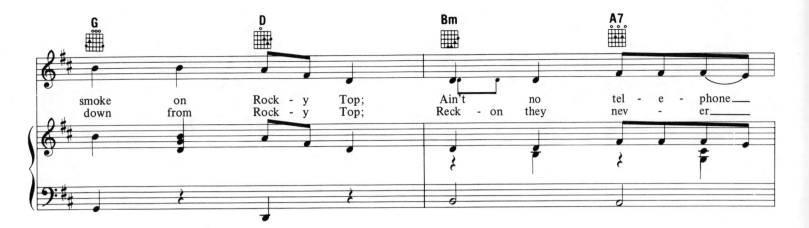

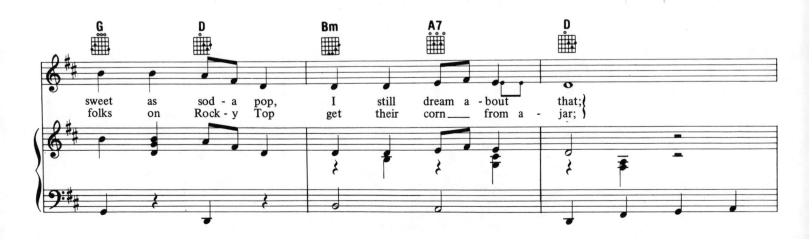

Chorus

Rock - y Top, you'll al - ways be home sweet home to

me; Good ol' Rock - y Top;

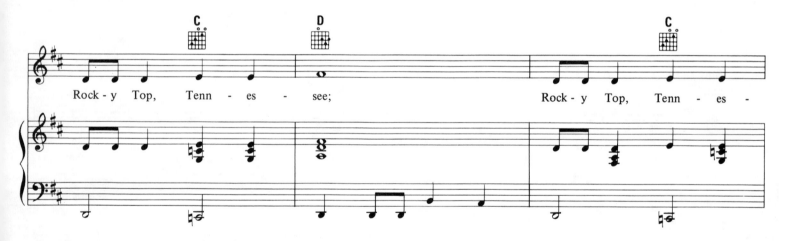

Rock - y Top, Tenn - es - see; Rock - y Top, Tenn - es -

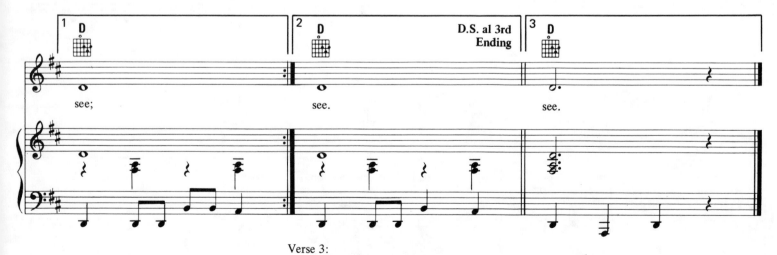

see; see. see.

Verse 3:
I've had years of cramped-up city life
Trapped like a duck in a pen;
All I know is it's a pity life
Can't be simple again. (Chorus)

I KNOW A HEARTACHE WHEN I SEE ONE

Words and Music by CHARLIE BLACK,
RORY BOURKE & KERRY CHATER

Look at who the winds blow-ing up the road
There was a time I was a true be-liev-er,

shin-ing like the north-ern star. Act-ing like the an-swer to
your love was the on-ly way; Well, you can save all your sweet talk-ing for
los-er is the one who cries; And when you've cried like a ba-by and you've

TEDDY BEAR

Words and Music by DALE ROYAL,
BILLY JOE BURNETTE, RED SOVINE
and TOMMY HILL

Moderately Bright

*Repeat Ad Lib and
Fade after Recitation*

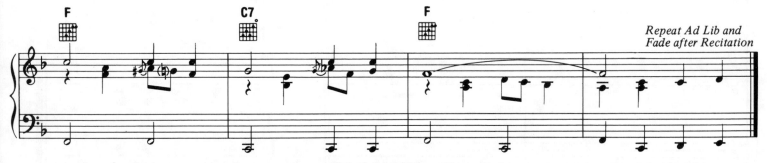

(Recitation:) I was on the outskirts of a little southern town; trying to reach my destination before the sun went down......The CB was blaring away on channel 19...when there came a little boy's voice on the radio line...... He said: "Breaker 19!...Is anyone there? Come on back, truckers...and talk to Teddy Bear!"......I keyed the mike and said: "You got it, Teddy Bear!" And a little boy's voice came back on the air......"Preciate the break,...... Who we got on that end?"...... I told him my handle and he began:......

"I'm not supposed to bother you fellows out there......Mom says you're busy and for me to stay off the air......But you see, I get lonely and it helps to talk... 'cause that's all I can do....I'm crippled,.....I can't walk!!!"

I came back and told him to fire up that mike......and I'd talk to him as long as he liked......"This was my dad's radio" the little boy said....."But I guess it's mine and mom's now, 'cause my dad's dead!"

"He had a wreck about a month ago..He was trying to get home in a blinding snow....Mom has to work now, to make ends meet...and I'm not much help with my two crippled feet!"

"She says not to worry...that we'll make it alright...But I hear her crying sometimes late at night......There's just one thing I want more than anything to see......Aw, I know you guys are too busy to bother with me!"

"But my dad used to take me for rides when he was home...but that's all over now, since my daddy's gone..."...Not one breaker came on the old CB as the little crippled boy talked with me..I tried to swallow a lump that wouldn't stay down......as I thought about my boy back in Greenville Town.

"Dad was going to take mom and me with him later on this year....I remember him saying: 'Someday this old truck will be yours, Teddy Bear!'......But I know now I will never get to ride an 18 wheeler again......but this old bus will keep me in touch with all my trucker friends!"

"Teddy Bear's gonna back on out now and leave you alone 'cause it's about time for mom to come home......Give me a shout when you're passing through......and I'll surely be happy to come back to you!"

I came back and said: "Before you go, 10 - 10......what's you home 20, little CB friend?"......He gave me his address and I didn't once hesitate....this hot load of freight would just have to wait!

I turned that truck around on a dime and headed for Jackson Street, 229..... I round the corner and got one heck of a shock......18 wheelers were lined up for three city blocks!

Every driver for miles around had caught Teddy Bear's call....and that little crippled boy was having a ball......For as fast as one driver would carry him in, another would carry him to his truck and take off again.

Well, you better believe I took my turn riding Teddy Bear....and then carried him back in and put him down on his chair....And if I never live to see happiness again.....I saw it that day in the face of that little man.

We took up a collection for him before his mama got home.....Each driver said goodbye and then they were gone....He shook my hand with his mile-long grin and said: "So long, trucker....I'll catch you again!"

I hit the Interstate with tears in my eyes....I turned on the radio and got another surprise...."Breaker 19!" Came the voice on the air...."Just one word of thanks from Mama Teddy Bear!"

"We wish each and every one a special prayer for you....you made a little crippled boy's dream come true.....I'll sign off now, before I start to cry....... May God ride with you......10 - 4......and goodbye!"

CHARLOTTE'S WEB

Words and Music by JOHN DURRILL,
CLIFF CROFFORD and SNUFF GARRETT

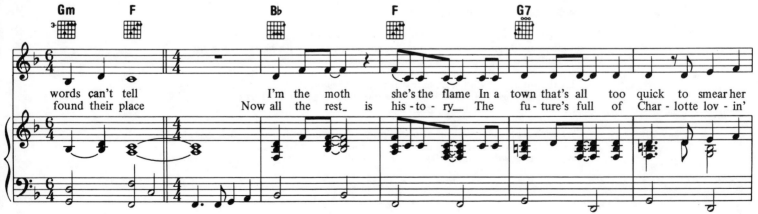

(There'll Be)
PEACE IN THE VALLEY
(For Me)

Words and Music by
THOMAS A. DORSEY

Moderato

Verse

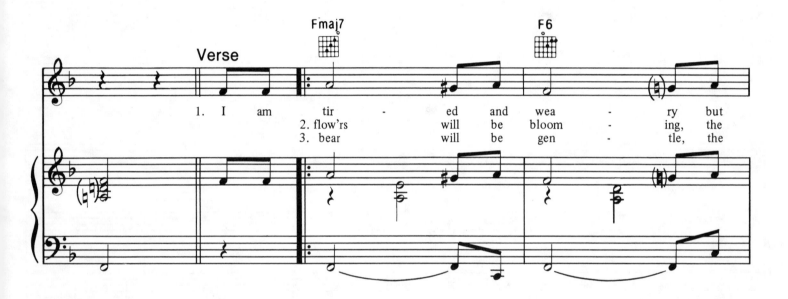

1. I am tir - ed and wea - ry but
2. flow'rs will be bloom - ing, the
3. bear will be gen - tle, the

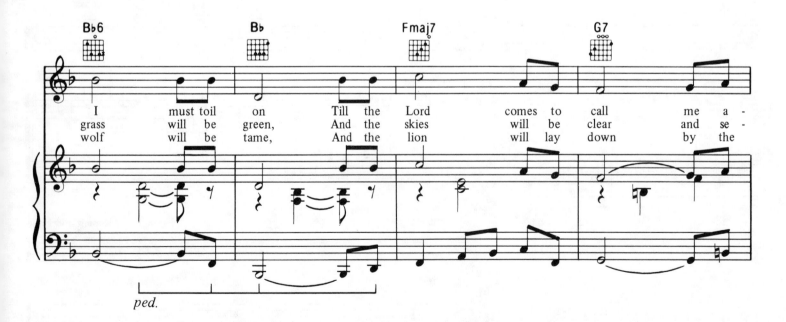

I must toil on Till the Lord comes to call me a -
grass will be on green, And the skies will be clear and se -
wolf will be tame, And the lion will lay down by the

ped.

Verse 4

4. No head-aches or heart-aches or misunderstands
   No confusion or trouble won't be
   No frowns to defile just a big endless smile,
   There'll be peace and contentment for me.

YOU'RE MY BESTEST FRIEND

Words and Music by MAC DAVIS

Lively

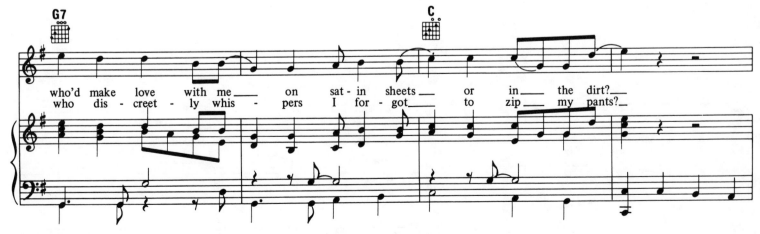

You babe, ___ You're My Best - est Friend. And
You babe, ___ You're My Best - est Friend.

who comes down bails me out ___ when I get in a jam. And
Who can be as gen - tle as ___ a spar - row in my hand. ___

helps me tell the po - lice where I ___ live and who I am? ___ And
Mean - er than a junk - yard dog when shes fight - in' for her man? ___ And

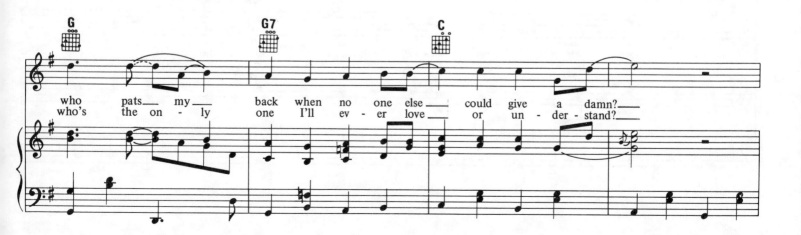

who pats my ___ back when no one else ___ could give a damn? ___
who's the on - ly one I'll ev - er love ___ or un - der - stand? ___

EVERY WHICH WAY BUT LOOSE

Words and Music by STEPHEN DORFF,
MILTON BROWN and SNUFF GARRETT

Medium Country

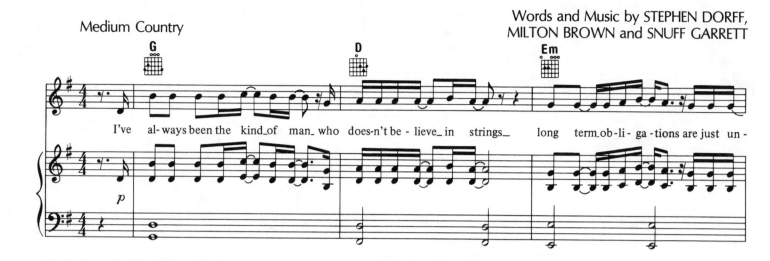

I've al-ways been the kind of man who does-n't be-lieve in strings long term ob-li-ga-tions are just un-

-ne-ces-sar-y things But girl you've got me think-in' while I'm drink-in' one more beer If I'm

head-ed for a heart-ache then why the hell am I still here I'm test-ing my re-sis-tance and it's
comes up in the mor-nin' it should

wear-in' might-y thin I've got the feel-ing I should leave be-fore the roof caves in My
find me some-place new But right this min-ute all I want is to lay here next to you Those

BEERS TO YOU

Words and Music by STEPHEN H. DORFF,
JOHN DURRILL, SANDY PINKARD and SNUFF GARRETT

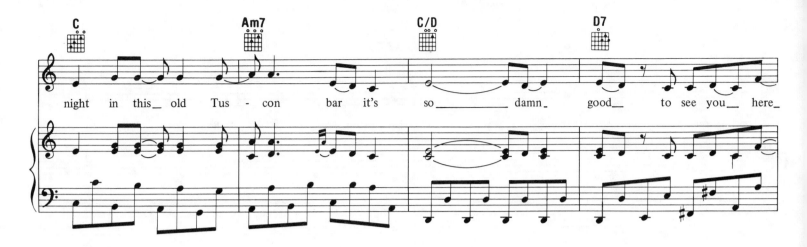

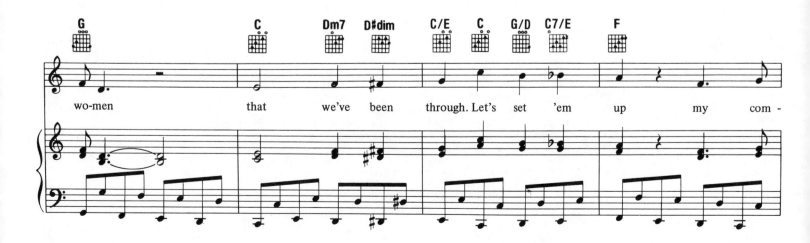

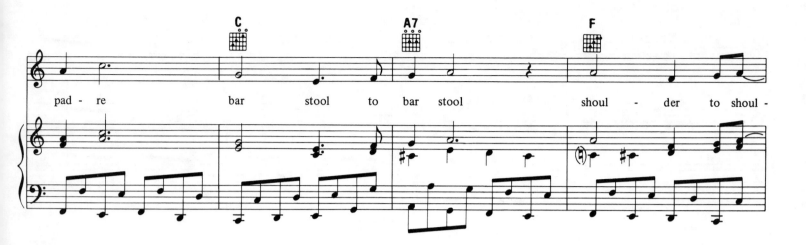

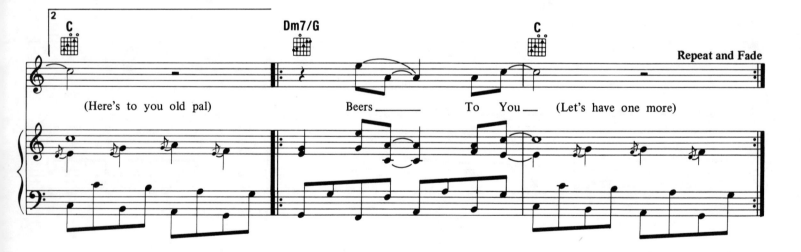

2. Do you remember back in Phoenix when we walked into that fight?
We whipped them local boys then bought 'em drinks all night.
And when my lovin' wife left for points unknown you were there to fill my glass.
It proved to me a womans love can fade but the taste of Coors
and a good friend always lasts.

Ad libs for tag: Hey Ray, let's have one more
O.K. Clint, but it's my turn to buy
Well then we'll have two more Beers To You.

THE LONG BLACK VEIL

Words and Music by MARIJOHN WILKIN
and DANNY DILL

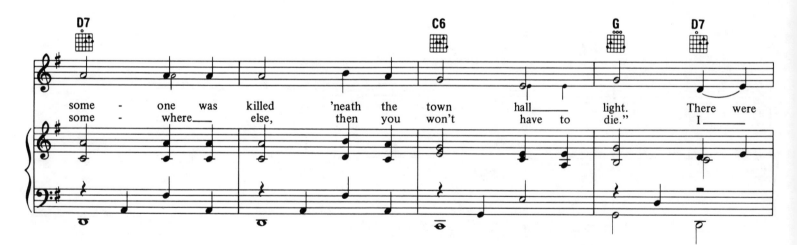

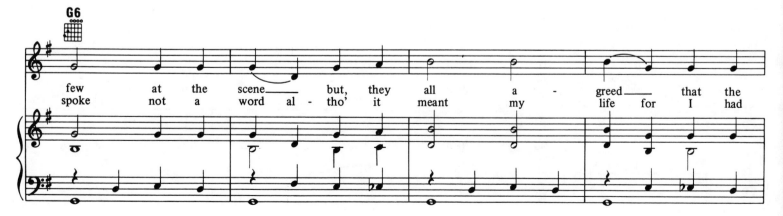

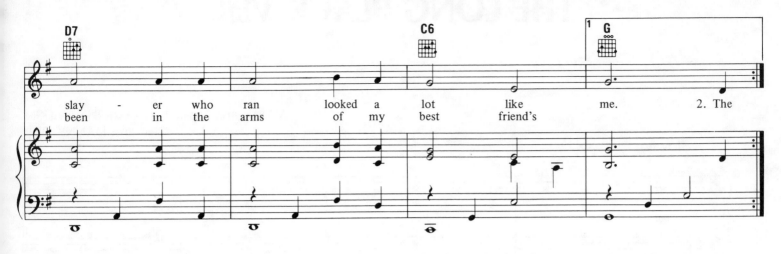

slay - er who ran looked a lot like me. 2. The
been in the arms of my best friend's

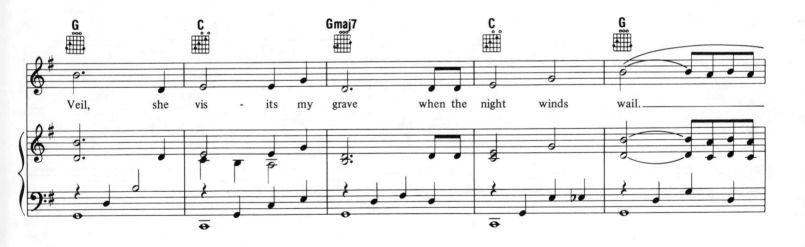

wife She walks these hills in a Long Black

Veil, she vis - its my grave when the night winds wail.

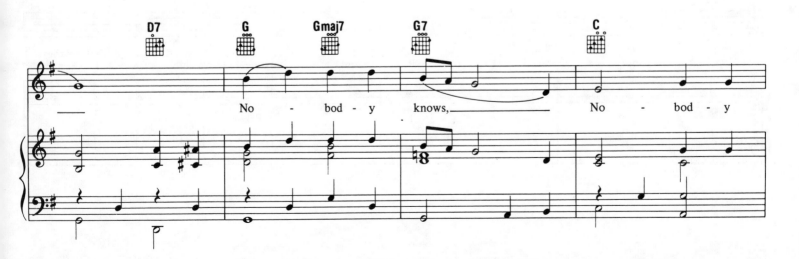

No - bod - y knows, No - bod - y

DADDY SANG BASS

Words and Music by CARL PERKINS

Moderately fast

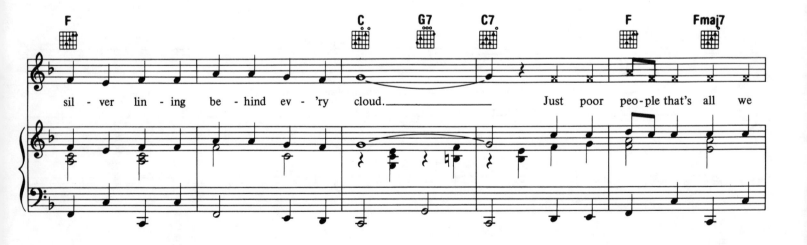

I re-mem-ber when I was a lad, times were hard and things were bad; But there's a
sil-ver lin-ing be-hind ev-'ry cloud._____ Just poor peo-ple that's all we

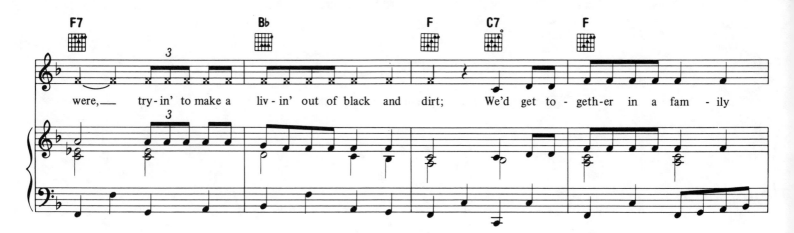

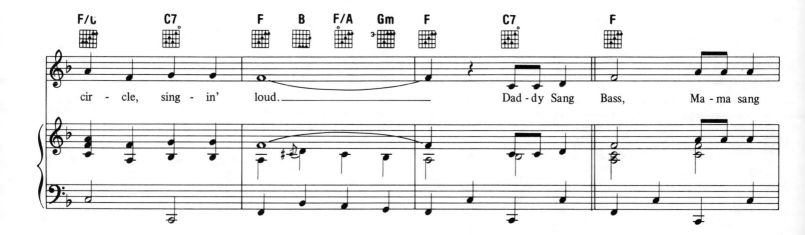

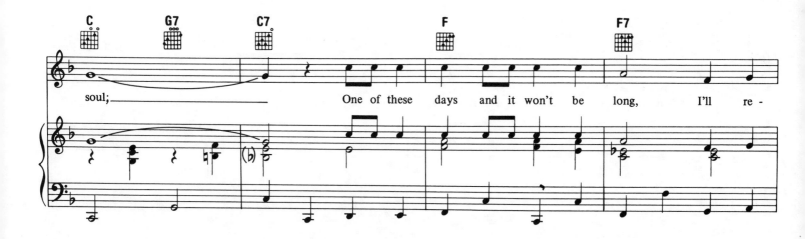

join them in a song; I'm gon-na join the fam-i-ly cir-cle at the

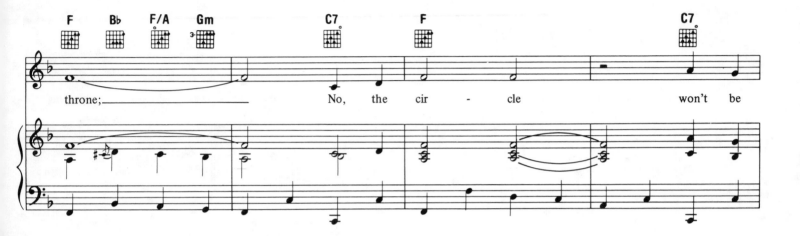

throne;_____ No, the cir - cle won't be

bro - ken bye and bye, Lord, bye and bye;_____

D.S. and Fade

_____ Dad-dy-'ll sing bass, Ma-ma-'ll sing ten - or, me and lit-tle bro-ther will join right

WILL THE CIRCLE BE UNBROKEN

Moderately

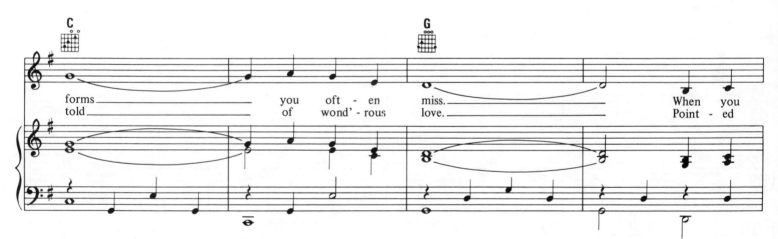

join_____ them in their bliss?_____ Will The
dwell_____ with Him a - bove._____

Cir - cle_____ Be Un bro - ken_____ by and

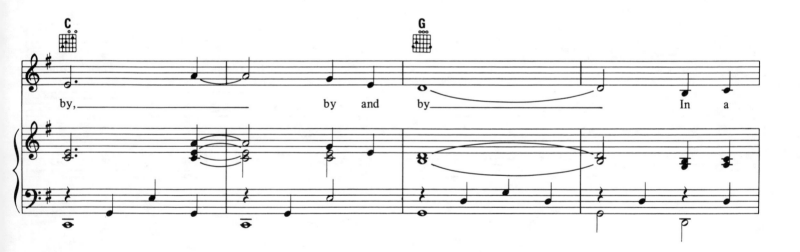

by,_____ by and by_____ In a

bet - ter_____ home a wait - ing_____ in the

BOUQUET OF ROSES

Words and Music by
STEVE NELSON & BOB HILLIARD

Slowly

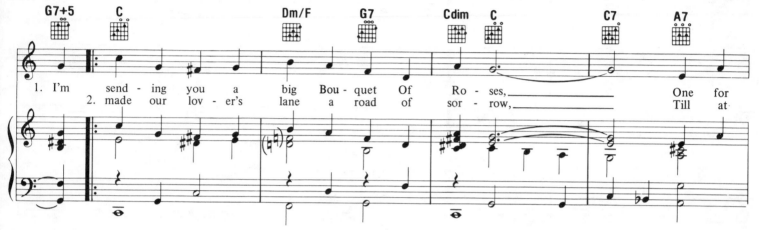

1. I'm send - ing you a big Bou - quet Of Ro - ses, _____ One for
2. made our lov - er's lane a road of sor - row, _____ Till at

ev - 'ry time you broke my heart, _____ And
last we had to say good - bye. _____ You're

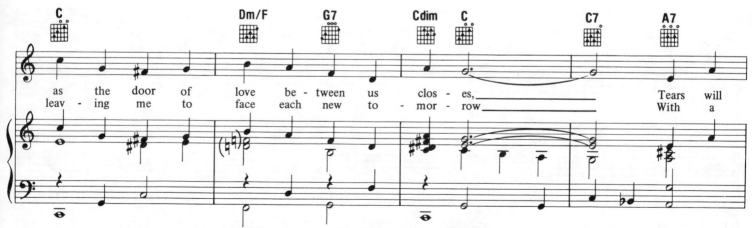

as the door of love be - tween us clos - es, _____ Tears will
leav - ing me to face each new to - mor - row _____ With a

SLOWLY

Words and Music by TOMMY HILL
and WEBB PIERCE

PERFECT FOOL

Country two-beat: Fast

Words and Music by DIANE PFEIFER

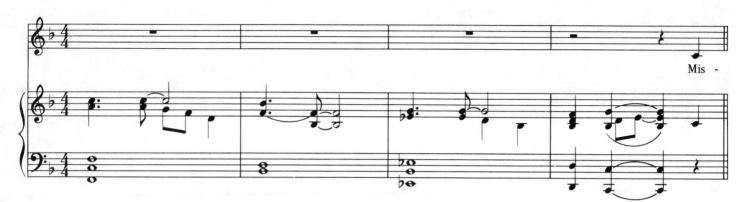

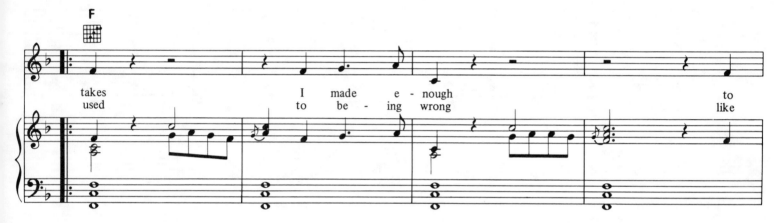

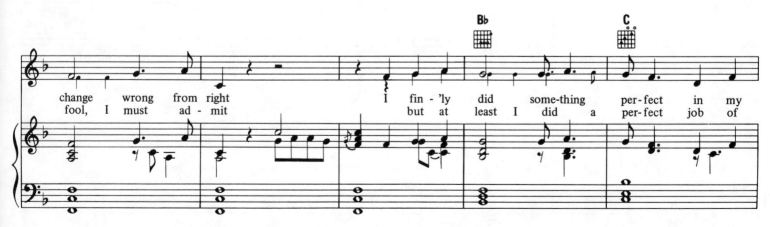

WAKE UP, LITTLE SUSIE

By BOUDLEAUX BRYANT
& FELICE BRYANT

Rock Tempo

Wake Up, Lit - tle Su - sie,___ wake up.

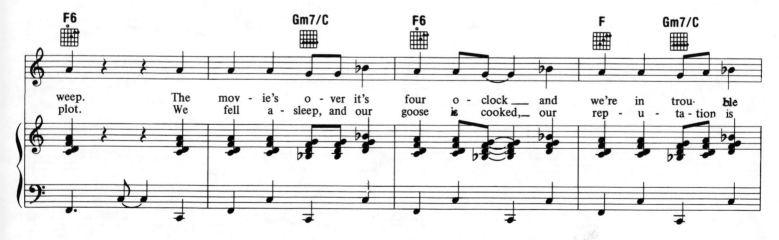

We've both been sound a - sleep,___ Wake Up,___ Lit - tle Sus - ie and
The mov - ie was-n't so hot,___ It did - n't have much of a

weep. The mov - ie's o - ver it's four o - clock ___ and we're in trou - ble
plot. We fell a - sleep, and our goose is cooked,___ our rep - u - ta - tion is

FLOWERS ON THE WALL

Words and Music by
LEWIS DE WITT

Moderato

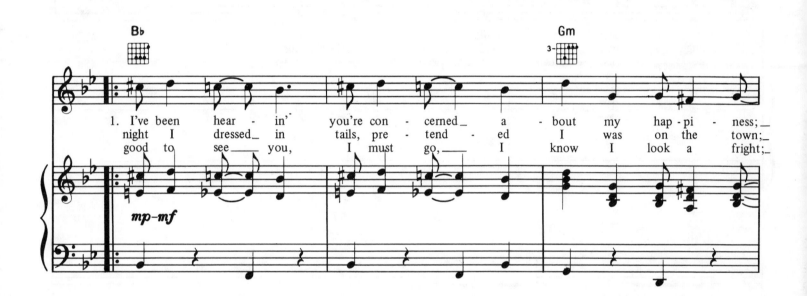

Bb   Gm

1. I've been hear-in' you're con-cerned a-bout my hap-pi-ness;
night I dressed in tails, pre-tend-ed I was on the town;
good to see you, I must go, I know I look a fright;

C7

But all that thought you're giv-in' me is
As long as I can dream it's hard to
An-y way my eyes are not ac-

N

ARE YOU SINCERE

Words and Music by WAYNE WALKER

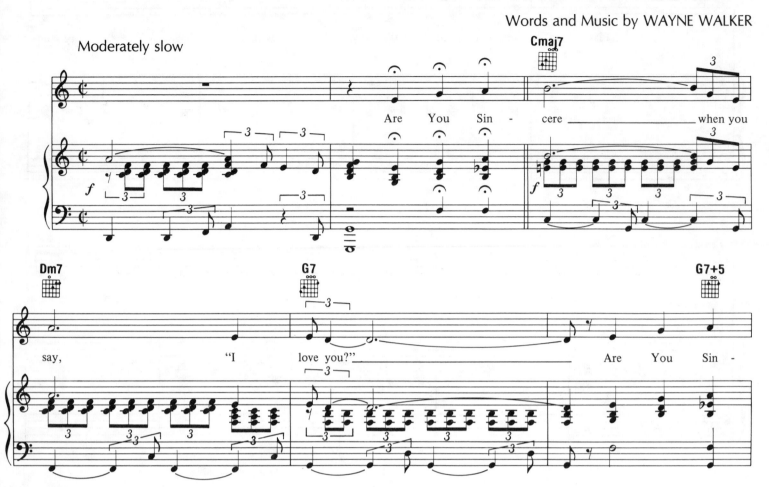

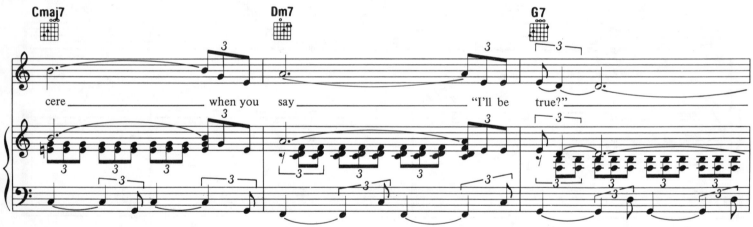

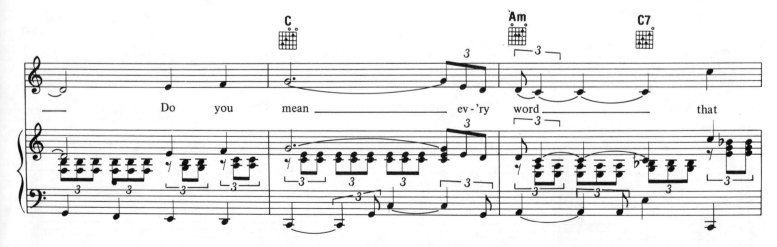

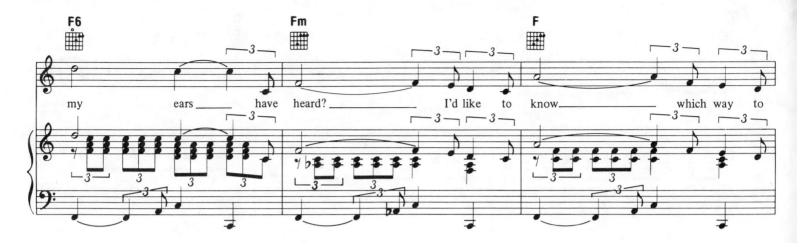

my ears ___ have heard? ___ I'd like to know ___ which way to

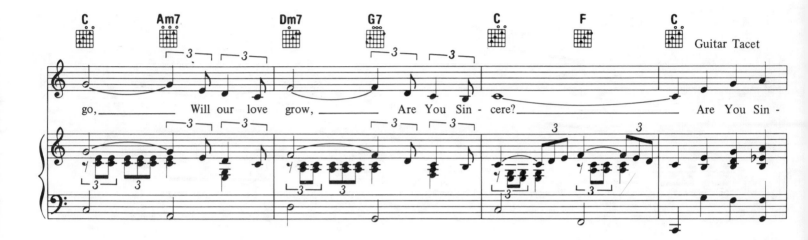

go, ___ Will our love grow, ___ Are You Sin - cere? ___ Are You Sin -

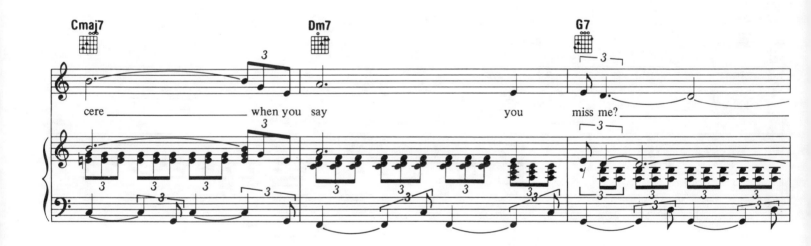

cere ___ when you say ___ you miss me? ___

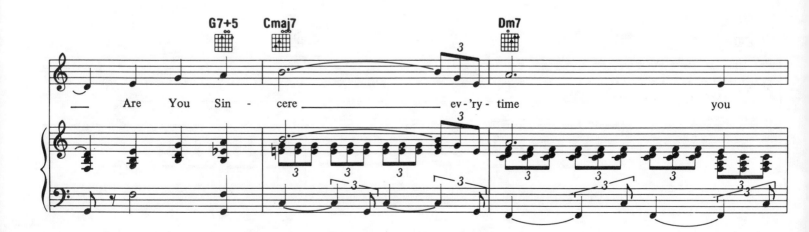

___ Are You Sin - cere ___ ev - 'ry - time ___ you

168

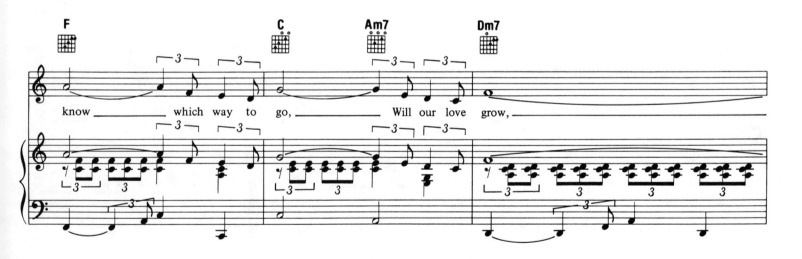

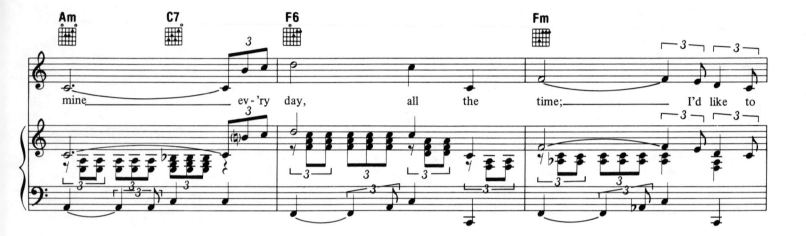

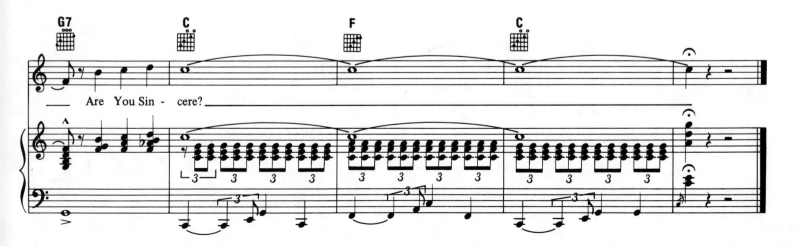

LAY DOWN SALLY

Words and Music by ERIC CLAPTON,
MARCY LEVY and GEORGE TERRY

Bright beat

There is noth - ing that ___ is wrong ___ in want - ing you ___ to stay ___

sun ain't near - ly on ___ the rise, ___ and we still got ___ the moon

long to see ___ the morn - ing light ___ col - or - ing ___ your face ___

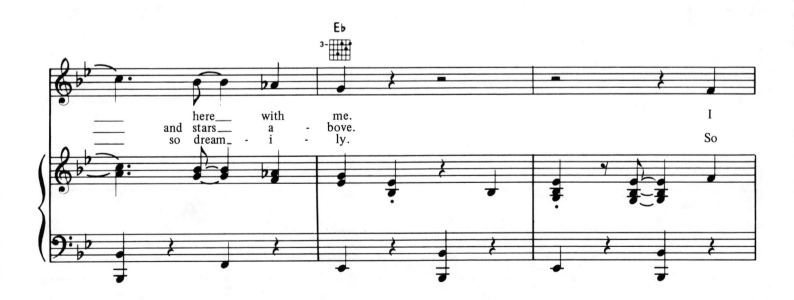

___ here ___ with me.

___ and stars ___ a - bove.

___ so dream - i - ly.

I

So

Don't you think__ you want__ some-one__ to talk__ to?

Lay Down, Sal - ly; no need to leave__ so soon.__

I've been try - ing all__ night long__ just to talk to you.__ The
I

Repeat and Fade

HERE I AM DRUNK AGAIN

Words and Music by DON WARDEN
and CLYDE BEAVERS

Easy Country two-beat

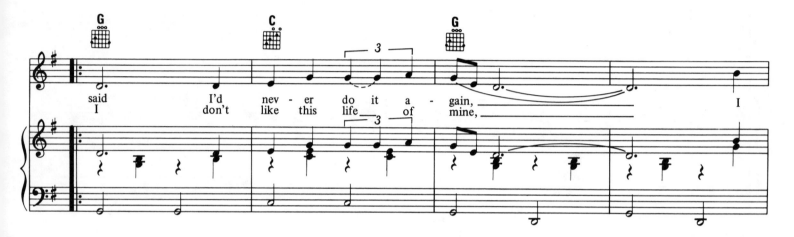

1. I said I'd nev-er do it a-gain, I don't like this life of mine, I

swore my ways I would mend. But you
drink-ing whis-key, beer and wine.

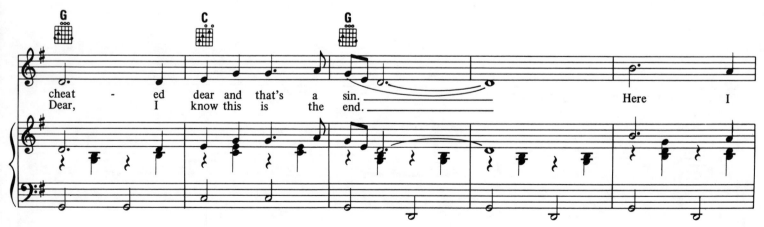

cheat-ed dear and that's a sin. Here I
Dear, I know this is the end.

THE WOMAN IN ME

Words and Music by
SUSAN MARIE THOMAS

Moderately Slow

Seems to me no mat-ter what I do___ I pick the
Can I help it if if feels___ good___ to have your

wrong time to do___ it___ In a min-ute I will be al-right_ if you will let me think_ it through___
arms wrapped a-round_me___ When you touch me I'm a lit-tle girl___ and there's so much that I___ still need___

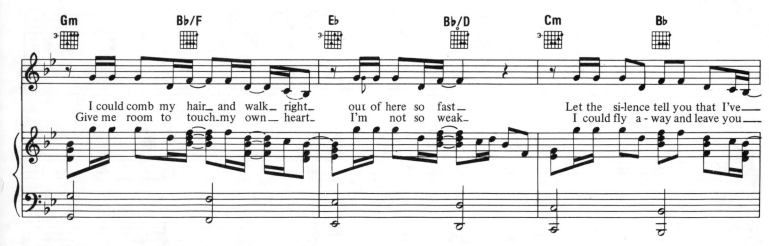

I could comb my hair___ and walk___ right___ out of here so fast___ Let the si-lence tell you that I've___
Give me room to touch_my own__ heart___ I'm not so weak___ I could fly a-way and leave you___

grown up at last___ {You'll nev-er break The Wo-man In Me___ though you might break a smile___You'll nev-er
A kiss on the cheek___

JEALOUSY

Words and Music by JIM ANGLIN

Moderately

Jeal - ous -

y; is there no cure? _____ Your dis-
of the air I breathe, _____ don't be a

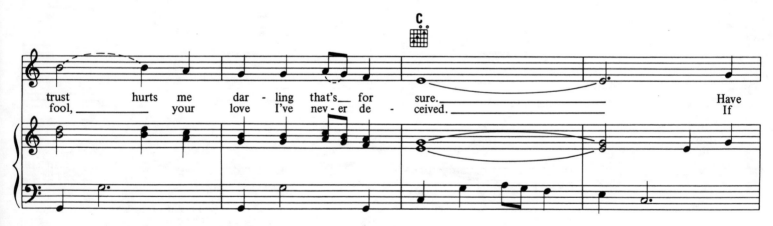

trust hurts me dar - ling that's_ for sure. _____ Have
fool, _____ your love I've nev - er de - ceived. _____ If

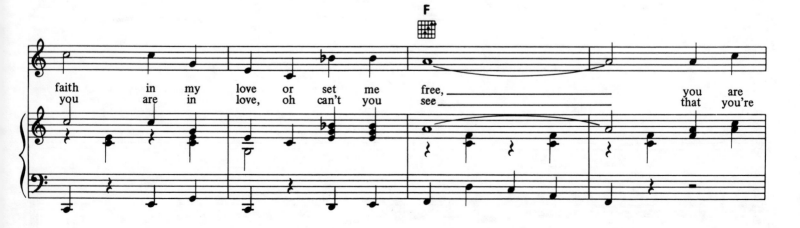

faith in my love or set me free, _____ you are
you are in love, oh can't you see _____ that you're

HOPELESSLY DEVOTED TO YOU

Words and Music by
JOHN FARRAR

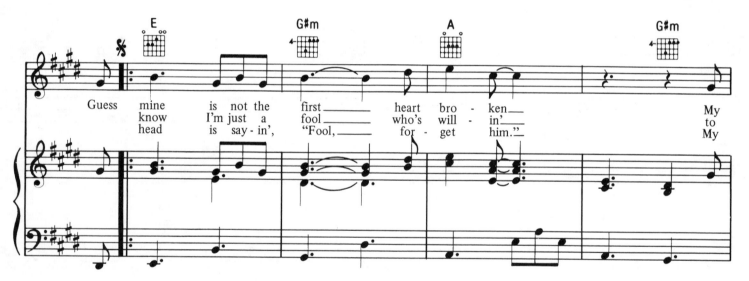

| E | G#m | A | G#m |

Guess mine is not the first_____ heart bro - ken_____ My
know I'm just a fool_____ who's will - in' to
head is say - in', "Fool,_____ for - get him." My

| F#m7 | B7 | E |

eyes are not the first_____ to cry. I'm
sit a - round and wait_____ for you. But,
heart is say - in', "Don't_____ let go.

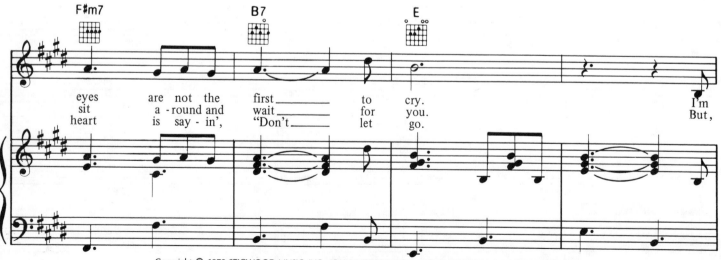

180

BIG BAD JOHN

Medium Country

Words and Music by JIMMY DEAN

Verse 1. Every morning at the mine you could see him arrive,
He stood six-foot-six and weighed two-forty-five.
Kind of broad at the shoulder and narrow at the hip,
And everybody knew you didn't give no lip to Big John!
(Refrain)

Verse 2. Nobody seemed to know where John called home,
He just drifted into town and stayed all alone.
He didn't say much, a-kinda quiet and shy,
And if you spoke at all, you just said, "Hi" to Big John!
Somebody said he came from New Orleans,
Where he got in a fight over a Cajun queen.
And a crashing blow from a huge right hand
Sent a Louisiana fellow to the promised land. Big John!
(Refrain)

Verse 3. Then came the day at the bottom of the mine
When a timber cracked and the men started crying.
Miners were praying and hearts beat fast,
And everybody thought that they'd breathed their last 'cept John.
Through the dust and the smoke of this man-made hell
Walked a giant of a man that the miners knew well.
Grabbed a sagging timber and gave out with a groan,
And, like a giant oak tree, just stood there alone. Big John!
(Refrain)

Verse 4. And with all of his strength, he gave a mighty shove;
Then a miner yelled out, "There's a light up above!"
And twenty men scrambled from a would-be grave,
And now there's only one left down there to save; Big John!
With jacks and timbers they started back down
Then came that rumble way down in the ground,
And smoke and gas belched out of that mine,
Everybody knew it was the end of the line for Big John!
(Refrain)

Verse 5. Now they never re-opened that worthless pit,
They just placed a marble stand in front of it;
These few words are written on that stand:
"At the bottom of this mine lies a big, big man; Big John!"
(Refrain)

TAKE MY RING OFF OF YOUR FINGER

Words and Music by BENNY JOY
and HUGH X. LEWIS

Easy Country feel

It

hurts ___ to share you with those oth - ers but it's
know I should walk right out and leave you

bet - ter than to have no love at all. When
an - y oth - er fool would have been gone.

you're not cheat - ing you're not hap - py so
Ev - 'ry night ___ you're un - faith - ful but

go on out and have your - self a ball. Just
I'll be wait - ing here when you come home.

Take My Ring Off Of Your Fin - ger, when your out

run - ning 'round on me. Dar - ling

tell them you're not mar - ried but don't ask me to set you

free. _____ I free.

DETROIT CITY

Words and Music by DANNY DILL
and MEL TILLIS

Hard-Driving rhythm

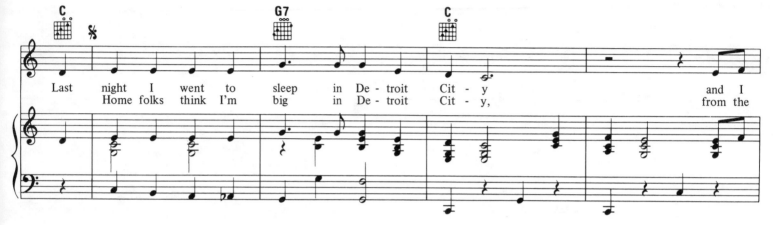

Last night I went to sleep in De-troit Cit-y, and I
Home folks think I'm big in De-troit Cit-y, from the

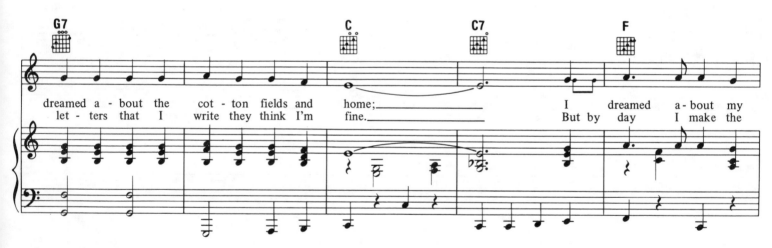

dreamed a-bout the cot-ton fields and home; I
let-ters that I write they think I'm fine. But by

dreamed a-bout my
day I make the

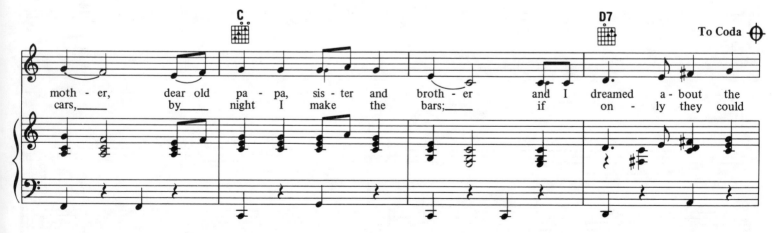

moth-er, dear old pa-pa, sis-ter and broth-er and I dreamed a-bout the
cars, by night I make the bars; if on-ly they could

To Coda ⊕

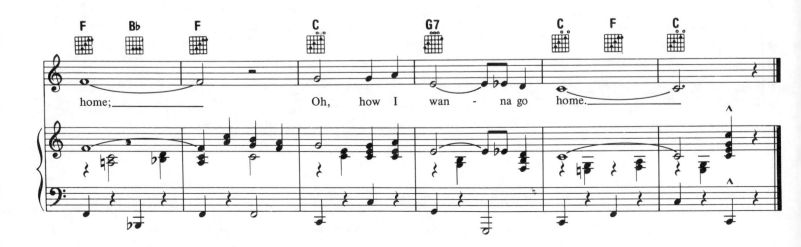

ROOM FULL OF ROSES

Words and Music by
TIM SPENCER

Moderato, with expression

Chorus

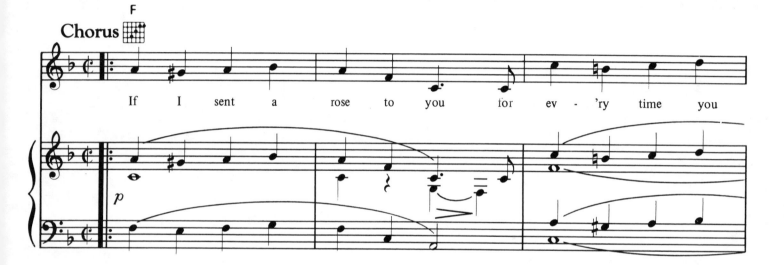

If I sent a rose to you for ev-'ry time you

made me blue, You'd have a Room Full Of Ros - es,

A BROKEN HEARTED ME

Words and Music by
RANDY GOODRUM

Moderately

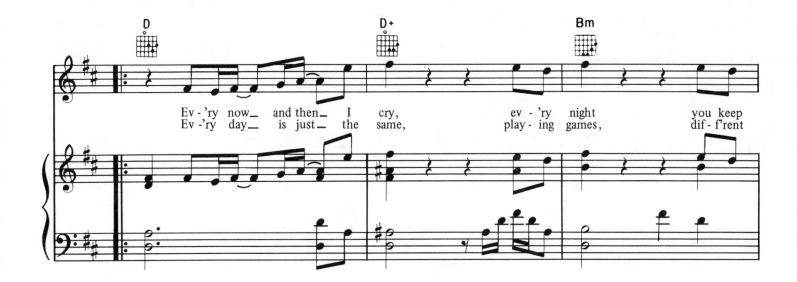

Ev-'ry now__ and then__ I cry, ev-'ry night you keep
Ev-'ry day__ is just__ the same, play-ing games, dif-f'rent

stay-in' on my mind.__ All my friends say I'll sur-vive,__ it just takes
lov-ers dif-f'rent names.__ They keep say-in' I'll sur-vive,__ it just takes

TUMBLING TUMBLEWEEDS

Words and Music by BOB NOLAN

Slowly

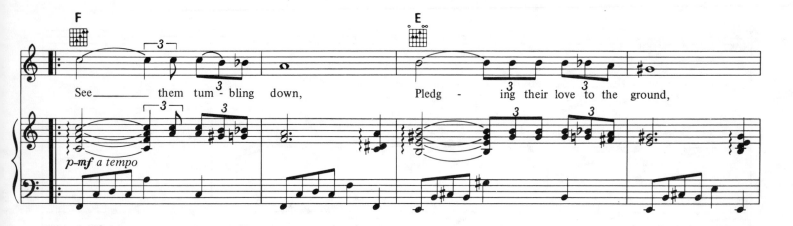

See____ them tum-bling down, Pledg - ing their love to the ground,

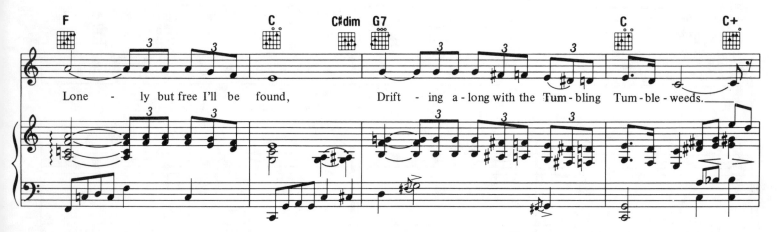

Lone - ly but free I'll be found, Drift - ing a - long with the Tum - bling Tum-ble-weeds.____

Cares____ of the past are be - hind, No - where to go, but I'll find

HONKY-TONK MAN

Words and Music by JOHNNY HORTON
TILLMAN FRANKS and HOWARD HAUSEY

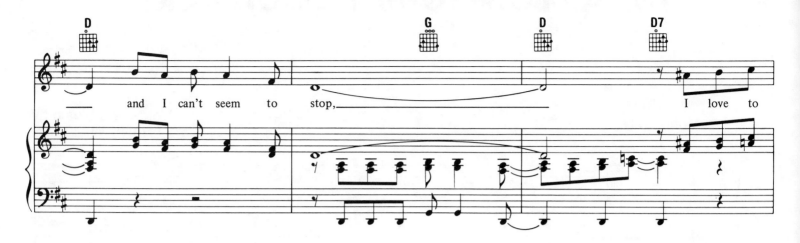

and I can't seem to stop,_____ I love to

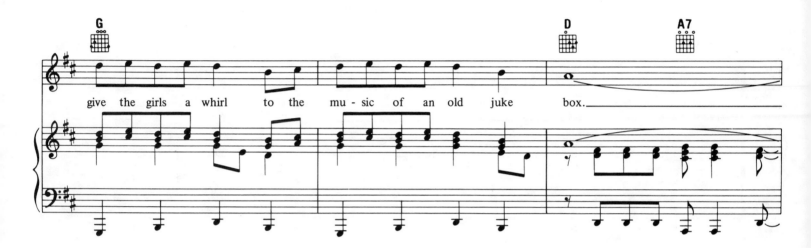

give the girls a whirl to the mu-sic of an old juke box._____

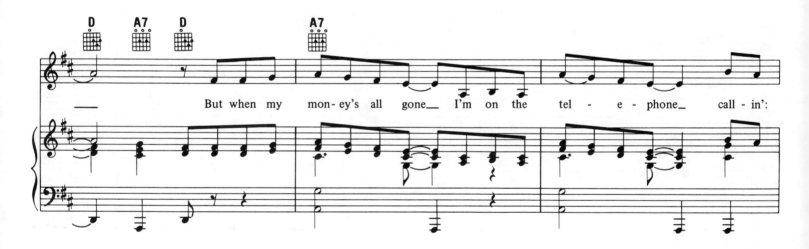

But when my mon-ey's all gone__ I'm on the tel - e - phone__ call-in':

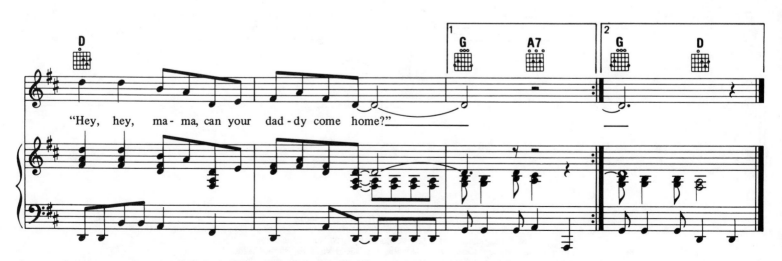

"Hey, hey, ma-ma, can your dad-dy come home?"_____

I'M SO LONESOME I COULD CRY

Words and Music by
HANK WILLIAMS

Moderately

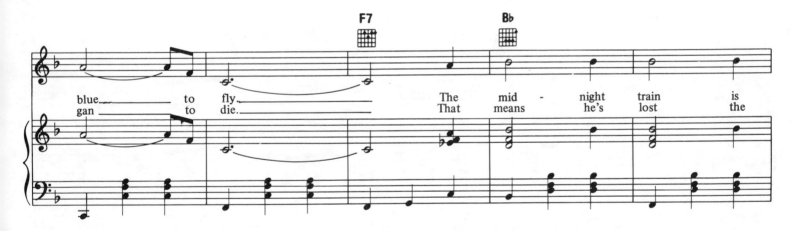

REST YOUR LOVE ON ME

Slow Ballad tempo

Words and Music by BARRY GIBB

May-be you don't know_me an-y-more than I know you, and I would-n't blame you if_ you walked a-way. I've been
Saw you in the cor-ner and the mo-ment I walked in saw your lone-ly face_ a-cross the room.

watch-ing you_ all eve-ning with the tear-drops in your eye and it touch-es me much more than I can say. You know I
No, I won't for-get_it and the way it might have been. Did you have to leave_ so soon? You know I

hate to think that some-one could have hurt some-one_like you, and if I was him_ I'd be right by your side._ }
hate to think that some-one could have loved you more than me, and at times like this_ I'd be right by your side._ }

Lay your trou-bles on__ my shoul-der, put your wor-ries in__ my pock - et, rest your love on me a - while.

Lay your trou-bles on__ my shoul - der, put your wor-ries in__ my pock - et. Rest your love on me a -

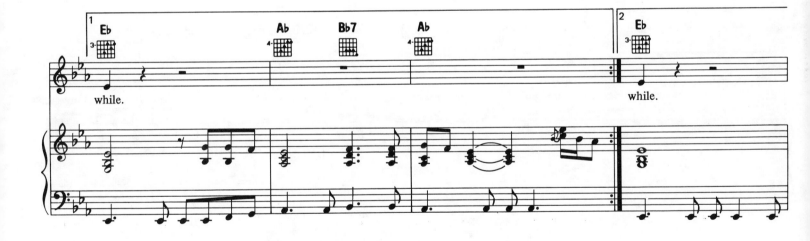

while. while.

How long must I wait, for the last train to be__ here, and the last chance to come.

Just to think that I___ was born too soon. How long, hon-ey, when the lov-in' don't come.___ I was

there when you left,___ just did-n't know_ how_ to be - gin. Lay your trou-bles on_ my shoul-

der, put your wor-ries in___ my pock - et, rest your love on me a - while. Lay your trou-bles on my shoul-

der, put your wor - ries in___ my pock - et rest your love on me a - while.

ANOTHER HONKY TONK NIGHT ON BROADWAY

Words and Music by STEVE DORFF,
MILTON BROWN and SNUFF GARRETT

Medium Country Western

sold my horse and sad - dle, rode the gray___ dog to New York. My gui - tar and fif - ty dol - lars 'tween

me and all___ a - lone.___ Found a job___ that pays___ O. K.___ But it costs twice as much to stay.___ So I'll just

buy my - self a beer___ and dream of home.

When___

Big City Miss Ruth Ann

Words and Music by THOMAS A LAZAROS

Ruth Ann, did you say that an-y-bod-y can be ex-act-ly what you want to man. Big Ci-ty Miss Ruth Ann.

Ruth Ann.

Well, I bet you're get-tin' lone-ly, on-ly you can cry, 'cause you're a big ci-ty girl now; So kiss the coun-try good-

bye.

Ruth Ann. Big Ci-ty Miss Ruth Ann.

A TEXAS STATE OF MIND

Words and Music by CLIFF CROFFORD,
JOHN DURRILL and SNUFF GARRETT

Country Blues Ballad

I'm in a Tex-as____ State Of____ Mind____ Been gone way too long____ this time_____ Cal-i-

for-nia's too damn far from you and that____ old lone star____ I'm in a Tex-as State____ Of____ Mind Your

dreams are much more than____ mine and each one leaves me far-ther be-hind____ I need to

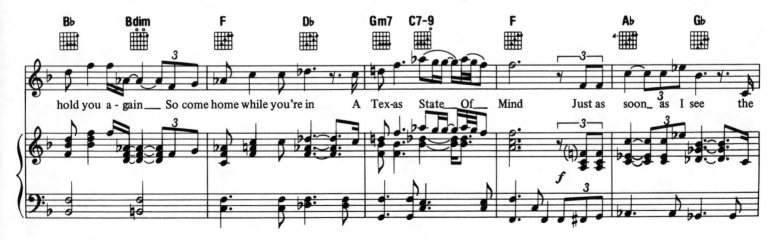

hold you a-gain____ So come home while you're in A Tex-as State____ Of____ Mind Just as soon____ as I see the

YOU'RE THE REASON
GOD MADE OKLAHOMA

Words and Music by
SANDY PINKARD and LARRY COLLINS

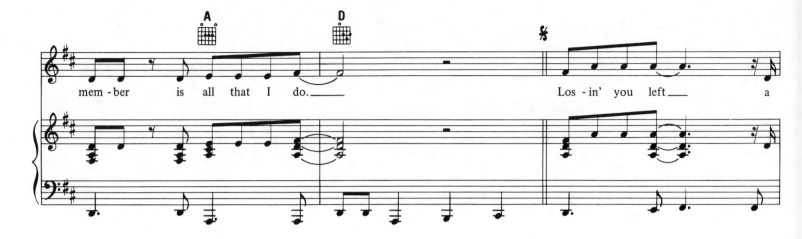

mem-ber is all that I do.____ Los-in' you left____ a

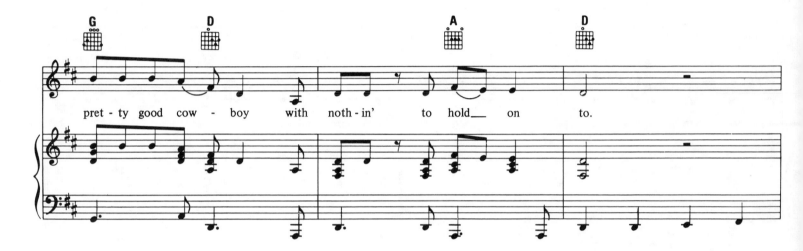

pret-ty good cow-boy with noth-in' to hold____ on to.

Sun-down came__ and I drove____ to town_____ and drank a drink__ or two._____

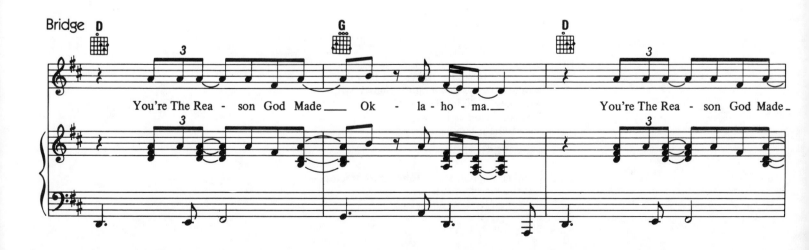

Bridge

You're The Rea - son God Made____ Ok - la - ho - ma.____ You're The Rea - son God Made__

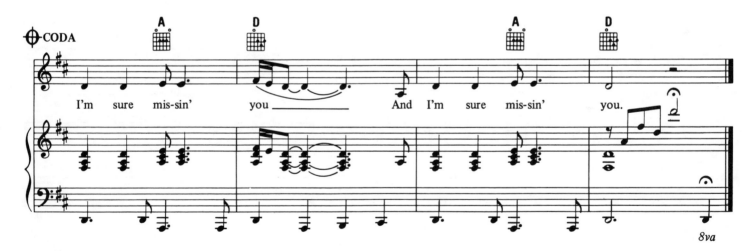

2. Here the city lights outshine the moon
I was just now thinking of you
Sometimes when the wind blows you can see the mountains
And all the way to Malibu
Everyone's a star here in L.A. County
You ought to see the things that they do.
All the cowboys down on the Sunset Strip
Wish they could be like you.
The Santa Monica Freeway
Sometimes makes a country girl blue

(BRIDGE)

3. I worked ten hours on a John Deere tractor,
Just thinkin of you all day....
I've got a calico cat and a two
room flat, on a
street in West L.A.

HARPER VALLEY P.T.A.

Moderately (with a heavy beat)

Words and Music by TOM T. HALL

I want to tell you all a stor-y 'bout a Har-per Val-ley wid-owed wife
note said, "Mis-ses John-son, you're wear-ing your dres-ses way too high;
hap-pened that the P. T. A. was gon-na meet that ver-y af-ter-noon;

Who had a teen-age daugh-ter who at-tend-ed, Har-per Val-ley Jun-ior
It's re-port-ed you've been drink-ing and a-run-nin' 'round with men and go-ing
They were sure sur-prised when Mis-ses John-son wore her mi-ni-skirt in-to the

high.
wild:
room.

Well her daugh-ter came home one af-ter-
And we don't be-lieve you ought to be a-
And as she walked up to the black-board, I

noon, and did-n't ev-en stop to play;
bring-ing up your lit-tle girl this way."
still re-call the words she had to say;

She said, "Mom, I got a note here from the
It was signed by the sec-re-tar-y,
She said, "I'd like to ad-dress this meet-ing

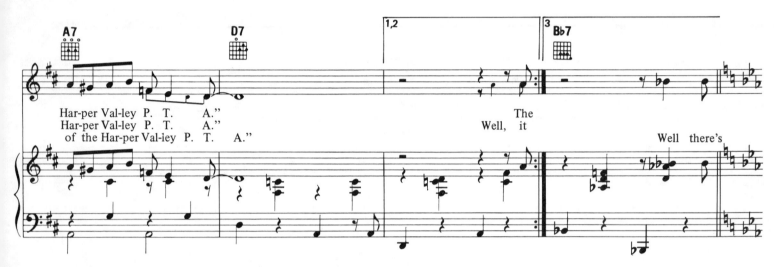

Har-per Val-ley P. T. A."
Har-per Val-ley P. T. A."
of the Har-per Val-ley P. T. A."

The
Well, it
Well there's

Bob-by Tay-lor, sit-tin there, and sev-en times he's asked me for a date;
Har-per could-n't be here 'cause he stayed too long at Kel-ly's Bar a-gain,

Miss-es Tay-lor sure seems to use a lot of ice when ev-er he's a-
And if you smell Shir-ley Tomp-son's breath, you'll find she's had a lit-tle nip of

PAPER ROSES

Words by JANICE TORRE
Music by FRED SPIELMAN

Moderately slow with expression

Verse

1. I re-al-ize the way your eyes de-ceived me_____ With ten-der looks that
2. (Your) pret-ty lips look warm and so ap-peal-ing,_____ They seem to have the
3. (I) thought that you would be a per-fect lov-er,_____ You seemed so full of

I mis-took for love;_____
sweet-ness of a rose;_____
sweet-ness at the start;_____

Girl {So take a-way the flow-ers that you
Boy {So throw a-way the flow-ers that I
But when you give a kiss there is no
But like a big red rose that's made of

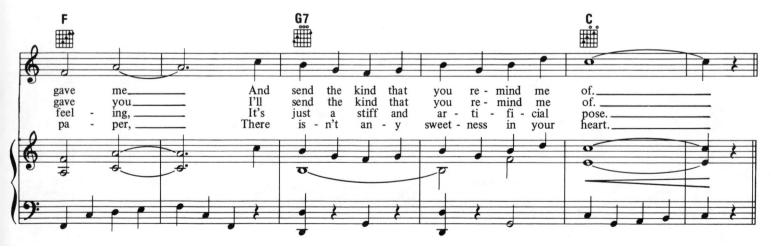

gave me_____
gave you_____
feel-ing,_____
pa-per,_____

And send the kind that you re-mind me of._____
I'll send the kind that you re-mind me of._____
It's just a stiff and ar-ti-fi-cial pose._____
There is-n't an-y sweet-ness in your heart._____

I JUST FALL IN LOVE AGAIN

Words and Music by
LARRY HERBSTRITT, STEPHEN H. DORFF,
GLORIA SKLEROV and HARRY LLOYD

LOVE ME TENDER

Words and Music by
ELVIS PRESLEY & VERA MATSON

Moderately slow

Verse

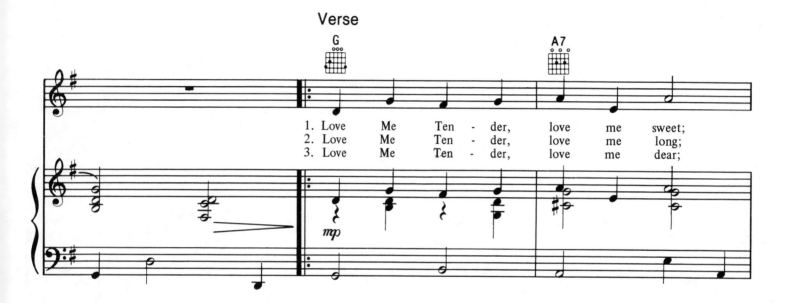

1. Love Me Ten - der, love me sweet;
2. Love Me Ten - der, love me long;
3. Love Me Ten - der, love me dear;

Nev - er let me go. You have made my
Take me to your heart. For it's made there that
Tell me you are mine. I'll be yours through

Chorus

life com - plete, And I love you so.
I be - long, And we'll nev - er part.
all the years, Till the end of time.

Love Me Ten - der, love me true, All my dreams ful -

fill. For, my dar - lin', I love you,

And I al - ways will. And I al - ways will.

EXTRA VERSE 4. When at last my dreams come true,
Darling, this I know:
Happiness will follow you
Everywhere you go.

LAURA
(What's He Got That I Ain't Got?)

By LEON ASHLEY
and MARGIE SINGLETON

Moderately

Lau-ra hold these hands and count my fin - gers,_____
Lau-ra see these walls that I built for you,_____

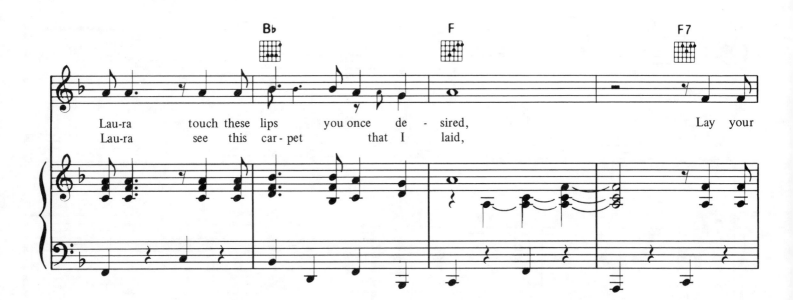

Lau-ra touch these lips you once de - sired,
Lau-ra see this car - pet that I laid,

Lay your

223

EVERY TIME YOU TOUCH ME

(I Get High)

Words and Music by CHARLIE RICH
and BILLY SHERRILL

Slowly

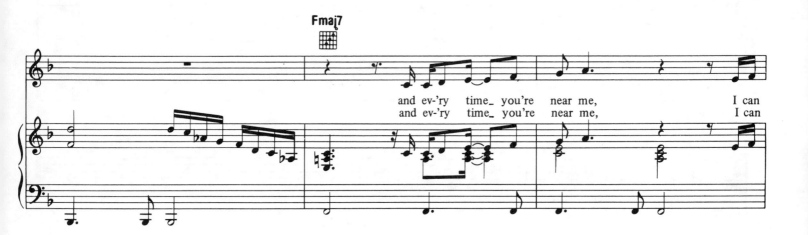

clouds and rain,
my skin,

way a-bove the hurt and pain, and
that's when I start to live a-gain, and 'cause with-

when you're gone, I fall down from the sky.
out your love, I'd lay right down and die.

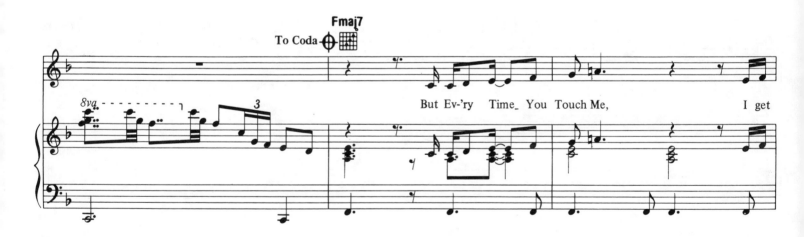

To Coda **Fmaj7**

But Ev-'ry Time_ You Touch Me, I get

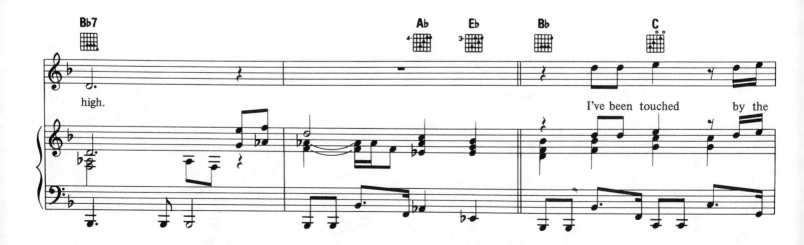

high.

I've been touched by the

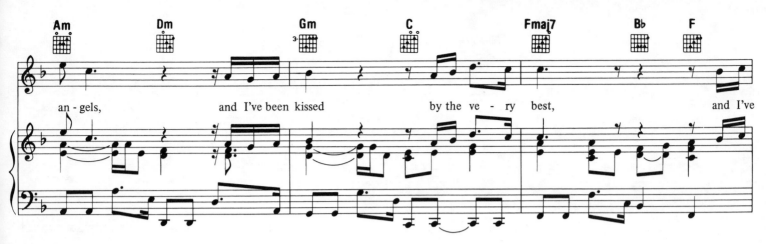

an - gels, and I've been kissed by the ve - ry best, and I've

been loved hard by quite a few, but af - ter you,

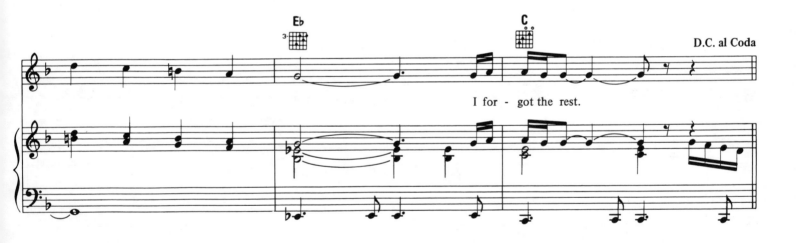

D.C. al Coda

I for - got the rest.

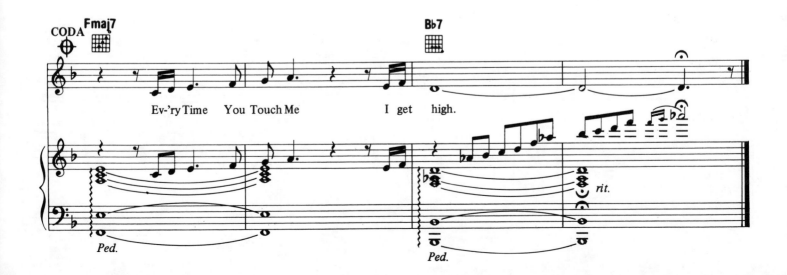

Ev-'ry Time You Touch Me I get high.

YOU NEEDED ME

Words and Music by
RANDY GOODRUM

Moderately

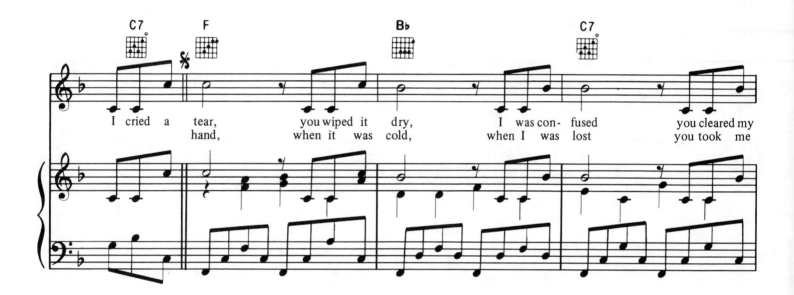

I cried a tear, you wiped it dry, I was con- fused you cleared my
hand, when it was cold, when I was lost you took me

mind, I sold my soul, you bought it back for me___ and held me
home You gave me hope, when I was at the end___ and turned my

SIXTEEN TONS

Words and Music by
MERLE TRAVIS

peo-ple say a man is made out of mud ___ A poor man's made out of
born ___ one ___ morn-in' when the sun did-n't shine ___ I picked up my shov-el and I
born ___ one ___ morn-in', it was driz-zl-ing rain ___ fight-in' and ___ trou-ble are
see ___ me ___ com-in' bet-ter ___ step a-side A ___ lot-ta men ___ did-n't ___ a

mus-cle and ___ blood, ___ Mus-cle and ___ blood ___ and ___ skin ___ and ___ bones ___ A
walked to the ___ mine, I load-ed Six- teen ___ tons ___ of ___ num-ber nine ___ coal And the
my mid-dle ___ name ___ I was raised ___ in a cane brake by an ole ___ ma-ma lion, Cain't no
lot-ta men ___ died ___ One ___ first of i-ron ___ the oth-er of ___ steel. If the

233

LEAVIN' ON YOUR MIND

Words and Music by WAYNE P. WALKER
and WEBB PIERCE

Very slow

If you've got Leav - in' On Your Mind,_____ Tell me now,____ get it
heart,_____ Tell me now,____ get it

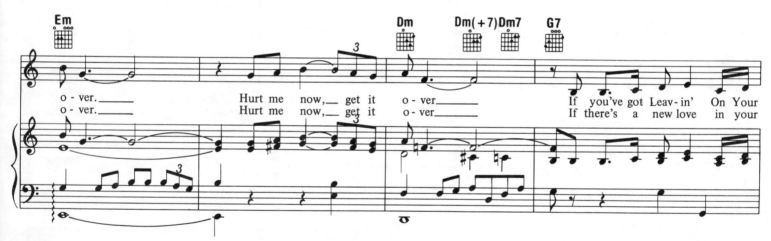

o - ver._____ Hurt me now,___ get it o - ver_____ If you've got Leav - in' On Your
o - ver._____ Hurt me now,___ get it o - ver_____ If there's a new love in your

Mind. If there's a new love in your heart._____ Don't leave me here in a

TAKE ME TO YOUR WORLD

Words and Music by
BILLY SHERRILL and GLENN SUTTON

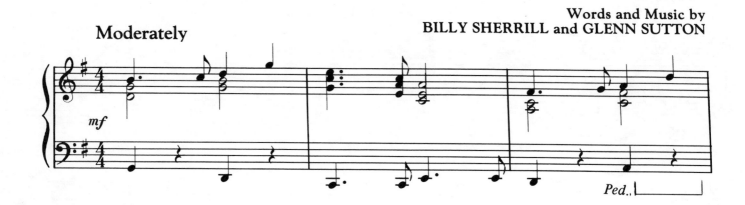

If you can find it in your heart to just for-give,

I'll come back and live the way you

STAND BY YOUR MAN

By TAMMY WYNETTE
& BILLY SHERRILL

I WALK THE LINE

Words and Music by JOHNNY CASH

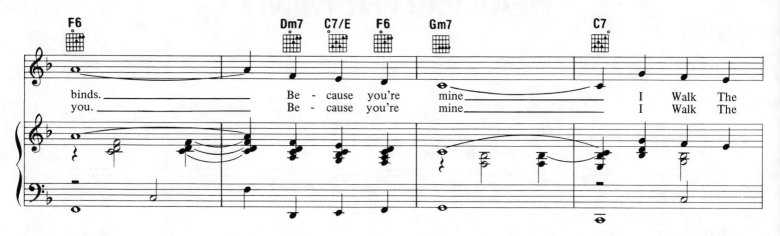

3. As sure as night is dark and day is light,
   I keep you on my mind both day and night.
   And happiness I've known proves that it's right.
   Because you're mine I Walk The Line.

4. You've got a way to keep me on your side.
   You give me cause for love that I can't hide.
   For you I know I'd even try to turn the tide.
   Because you're mine I Walk The Line.

5. I keep a close watch on this heart of mine.
   I keep my eyes wide open all the time.
   I keep the ends out for the tie that binds.
   Because you're mine I Walk The Line.

HEART OVER MIND

Easy two-beat

Words and Music by MEL TILLIS

CRYING IN THE CHAPEL

Words and Music by
ARTIE GLENN

Slowly, with expression

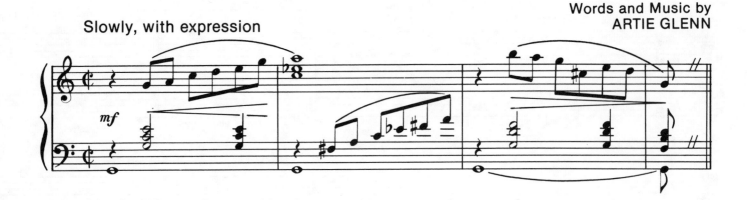

Chorus

1. You saw me Cry-ing In The Chap-el, _____ The tears I shed were tears of
(2. Ev -'ry sin - ner looks for) some - thing _____ That will put his heart at

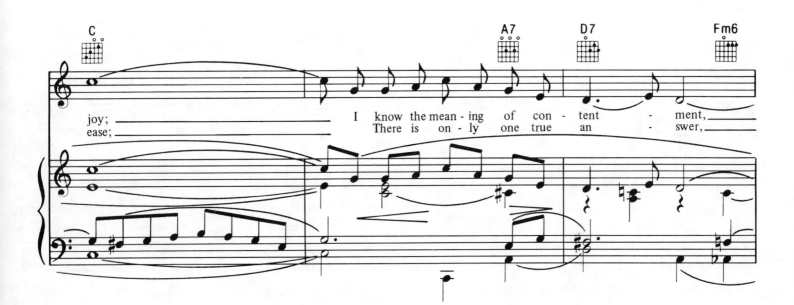

joy; _____ I know the mean - ing of con - tent - ment, _____
ease; _____ There is on - ly one true an - swer, _____

FUNNY FACE

By DONNA FARGO

Gently

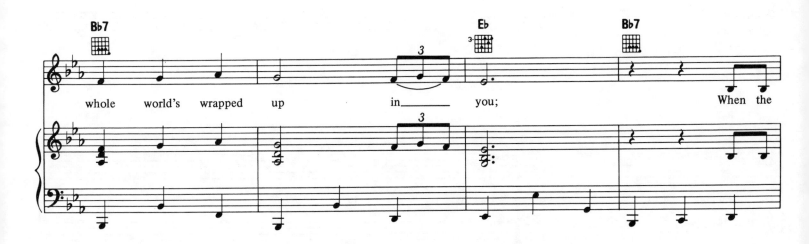

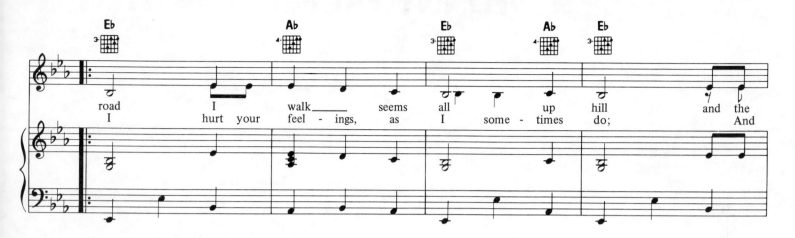

road I walk seems all up hill and the
I hurt your walk feel - ings, as I some - times do;

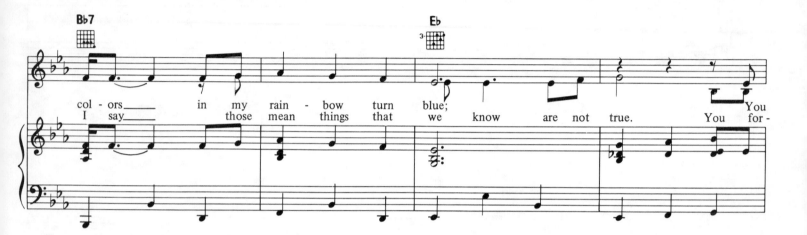

col - ors in my rain - bow turn blue; You
I say those mean things that we know are not true. You for -

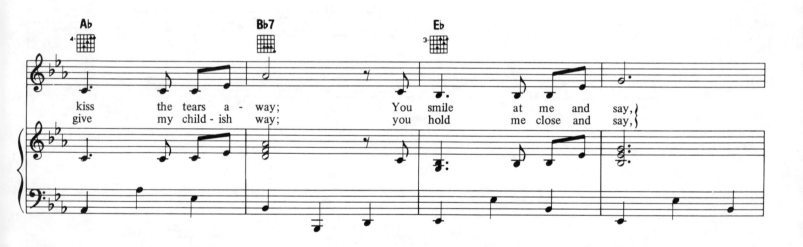

kiss the tears a - way; You smile at me and say,
give my child - ish way; you hold me close and say,

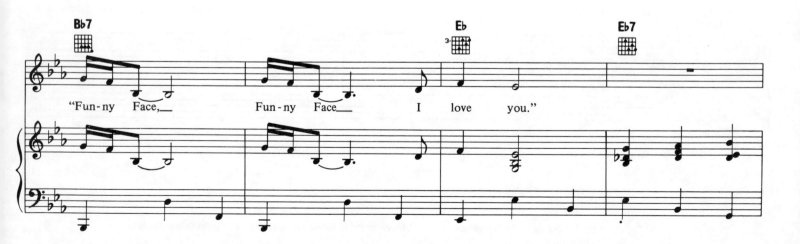

"Fun - ny Face, Fun - ny Face I love you."

Fun-ny Face___ I love you, Fun-ny Face___ I need you;

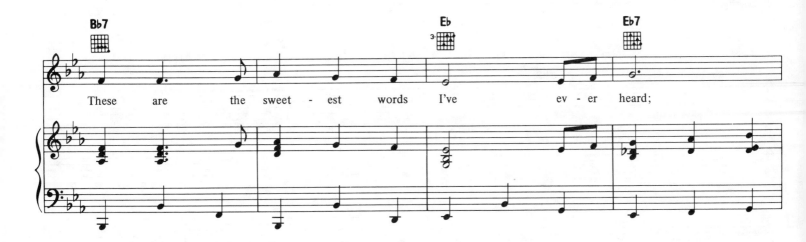

These are the sweet-est words I've ev-er heard;

Fun-ny Face___ don't leave me; Fun-ny Face,___ be-lieve me, my

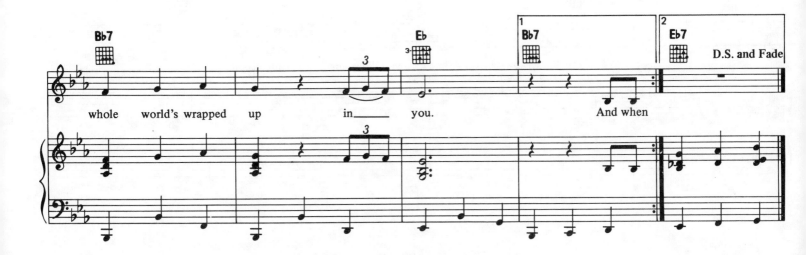

whole world's wrapped up in___ you. And when

COCA COLA COWBOY

Words and Music by S. PINKARD,
I. DAIN, S. DORFF and S. ATCHLEY

Medium Country Blues

I call col-lect on the phone___ You say you're tired and a-lone___
She said just leave me a-lone___ and let me hang up this phone___

but it sounds like some-one else___ is ly-in'___ there
'Cause he'll see me cry and think I'll still___ love___ you

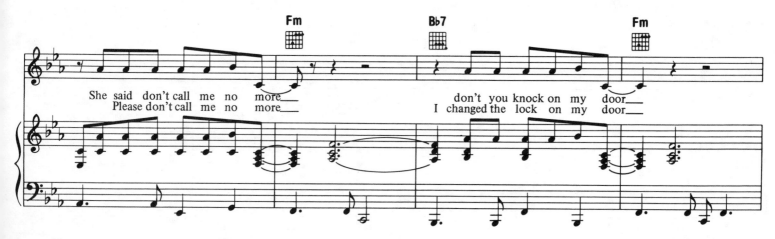

She said don't call me no more___ don't you knock on my door___
Please don't call me no more___ I changed the lock on my door___

It's too late now__ and I know__ you'll nev-er__ change
And it's time you un-der - stand__ that we are__ through

And she said

FALLEN ANGEL

Bouncing two-beat

Words and Music by WAYNE P. WALKER
WEBB PIERCE and MARIJOHN WILKIN

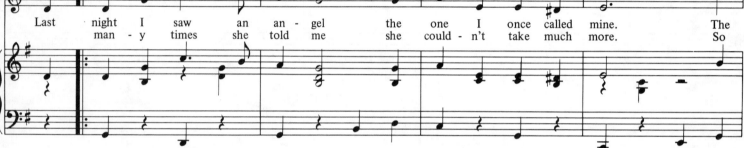

Last night I saw an an - gel the one I once called mine. The
man - y times she told me she could - n't take much more. So

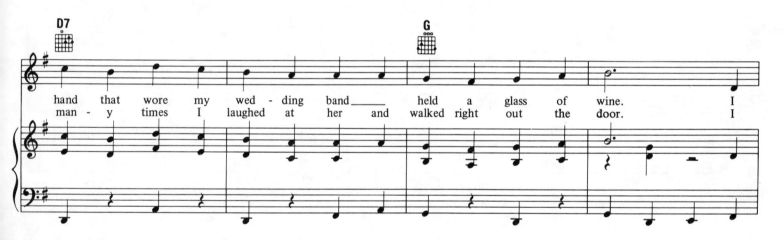

hand that wore my wed - ding band___ held a glass of wine. I
man - y times I laughed at her and walked right out the door. I

took her love for grant - ed. I wronged her night and day. I
was - n't wor - thy of her and now my an - gel's gone. The

drove my an - gel from me, and now she's gone a - stray. _____
de - vil took her from me and claimed her for his own. _____

She's just a Fall - en An - gel _____ but I don't blame her for it

all. She's just a Fall - en An - gel _____ and I'm the fool who made her

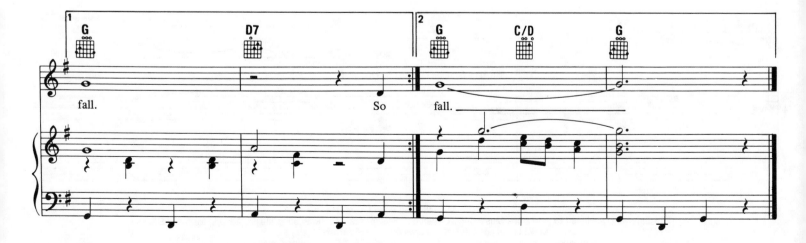

fall.   So fall. _____

HONKY TONK BLUES

Words and Music by
HANK WILLIAMS

MISERY AND GIN

Words and Music by JOHN DURRILL
and SNUFF GARRETT

Moderately slow, with expression

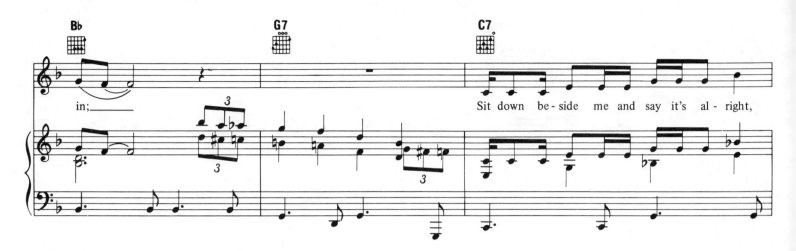

in;_____ Sit down be-side me and say it's al-right,

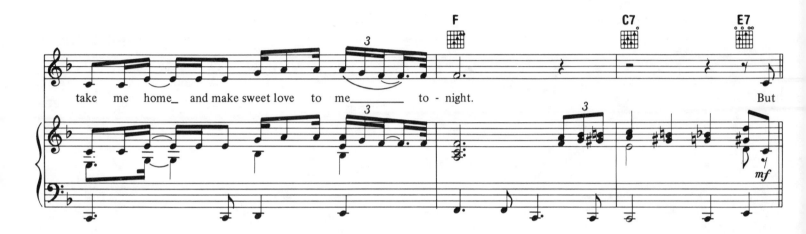

take me home_ and make sweet love to me_____ to - night. But

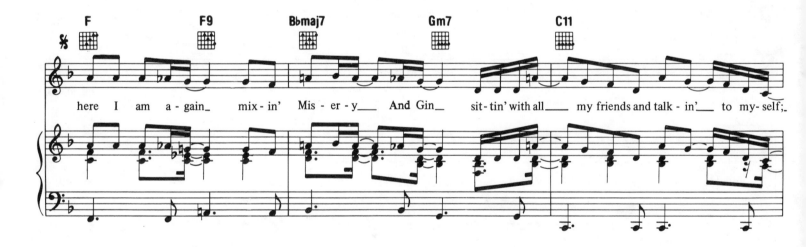

here I am a-gain_ mix-in' Mis-er-y___ And Gin___ sit-tin' with all____ my friends and talk-in'___ to my-self;

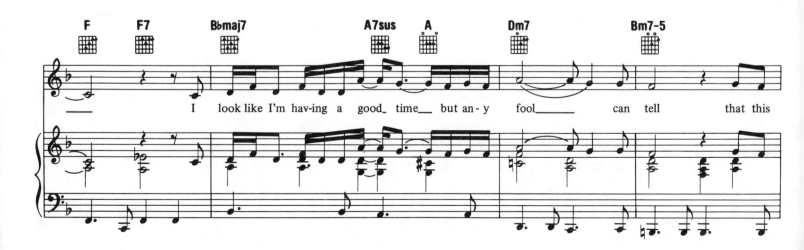

I look like I'm hav-ing a good_ time___ but an-y fool_____ can tell that this

Cow Patti

Words and Music by JIM STAFFORD

And you only had to kill her daddy once, to get that gal p.o.'d.

Courageously

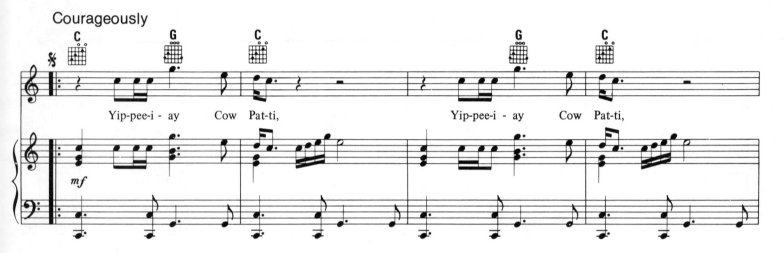

Yip-pee-i - ay Cow Pat-ti, Yip-pee-i - ay Cow Pat-ti,

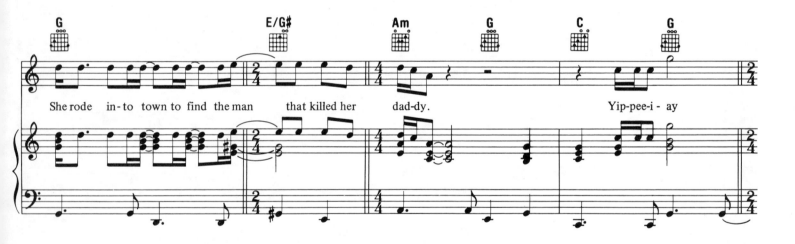

She rode in-to town to find the man that killed her dad-dy. Yip-pee-i - ay

Gloomily

(Spoken) Cow Patti, The killer hit the town at day break, ate the
The killer took a step toward

263

I ALMOST LOST MY MIND

Words and Music by
IVORY JOE HUNTER

Very slow

mf

F   Bb F C7 F   F7

1. When I lost my ba - by I Al - most Lost My Mind. I
2. pass a mil-lion peo - ple, I can't tell who I meet. I
3. went to see a gyp - sy And had my for - tune read.
4. I can tell you peo - ple, The news was not so good. Well

Bb   F

When I lost my ba - by, I Al - most Lost My Mind. My
pass a mil-lion peo - ple, I can't tell who I meet. 'Cause
went to see a gyp - sy, And had my for - tune read. I
I can tell you peo - ple, The news was not so good. She

C7+5   Bb/C   C7   F |1. |2. C7+5 F9

head is in a spin Since she left me be - hind.   2. I
my eyes are full of tears, Where can my ba - by be?   3. I
hung my head in sor - row When she said what she said.   4. Well,
said your ba - by has quit you, This time whe's gone for good.